The Consumer Guide to Horse Ownership and Purchase

By

Rob Liotti

Foreword by: Zack Mills, DVM

EQUINE CONSUMER
LIMITED
SINCE 1996

To Giovanna - Second year DVM candidate at Mississippi State University - for striving to achieve the highest level of excellence in veterinary medicine and for being my goddaughter. I am so proud of your journey.

A very special thank you to Zack Mills, DVM, for his foreword for this work.

To my beautiful Polish Arabian, *Rhythm King*. I miss you every day. Run free in Heaven.

And in memoriam - Dr. John P. Bradford, DVM (1954-2025) for his selfless decades of service caring for animals, including my own.

"God forbid I should go to any Heaven in which there are no horses."

- Robert B. Cunningham, 1917

Table of Contents

Foreword

by: Zack Mills, DVM

When Rob Liotti asked me to write the foreword for his book, I thought at first that he had picked the wrong man. I'm a small animal veterinarian, not an expert on horses. But then I realized why he had chosen me. His book is designed for a person who has never bought or owned a horse but wants to buy one for a child or him/herself - and I qualify as an expert in that field.

From that perspective, I can only say that this is the perfect book. And speaking as a veterinarian, I wish there were similar books for *all* pets.

I can't think of anything that this book does not cover such as ownership options, choosing your medical practitioner and farrier, instruction and training, legal and business aspects of buying a horse, and more. This is probably the first book about buying a horse that covers it all.

While the book is comprehensive, it's also easy to read. Liotti warns that horse ownership *"is more complicated than one may think,"* but assures us that *"in the following text, you will obtain a clearer understanding of what is involved in equine ownership."* I can assure you that he keeps that promise.

But if I had to say what I admire most about this book (and coincidentally about the author) I would have to say it is his loud, clear, and unrelenting message that owning a horse is not a right, but a privilege. And it's an expensive one at that—expensive— especially in regard to commitment and time, as well as money. As Liotti puts it: *"Commitment and dedication are the operative terms here."*

Liotti and I both have seen too many Christmas puppies and Easter bunnies who ended up in the Humane Shelter, because they had been purchased without the full understanding or commitment to what it means to be a pet owner. I believe we share a belief that a horse is a living, breathing animal that needs and deserves an owner's full attention to having a quality life.

That's why I believe every parent who is thinking of buying a pet horse for a child *must* read this book. As Liotti points out: *"I have seen few children who actually handle the responsibility well."*

If you are thinking of giving a child major responsibility for a pet horse, this book may help you make a wise purchase - or it may help you make the wise and proper decision not to make a purchase at all. In fact, my wife and I were in the latter category. This book helped us realize that our children were much too busy for the responsibility of horse ownership—and so were we.

To paraphrase a cynical old saying about boat ownership: *The two greatest days of owning a boat (or a horse) are the day you buy it and the day you sell it.*

Liotti set out to prove that old saying wrong—to help people make responsible, smart business decisions in buying and keeping a horse. He reminds us that buying is as much an art as selling and guides us through all the steps to take proper ownership of a 1,500-pound friend and companion.

The book is, in short, an excellent reference.

Introduction

Back in the early 1990's, I became a first-time horse owner. While I was full of ambition and vigor, this new venture was one that was almost completely foreign to me. In hindsight, I didn't consider the many issues that would later have such an impact on the process, responsibility, and realm of horse ownership. Moreover, as with any new project, I was somewhat overwhelmed with the novelty of my newly found friend and family member. It is quite easy to imagine that you will be equally overtaken with the prospect of horse ownership, yourself. In addition, I can relate to all the anxiety, apprehension, and excitement that you are feeling as you take this opportunity to consider making that most important purchase.

You've made one very responsible and prudent decision by opening this book and making careful examination of your desires and expectations regarding horse ownership. By no means is this book the answer to every proposed question surrounding the equine industry, but I can assure you that in the following text you will obtain a much clearer understanding of what *is* involved in equine ownership. To say the least, horse ownership is more complicated than one may think and warrants some preliminary study and due diligence.

While it is true that some could say that the information that I provide is too cautious or the approach too tactical, one cannot dispute that the information is factual. In my opinion, a far too informal approach to such an important transaction is an invitation to poor results because this transaction can be somewhat permanent. In other words, your responsibility is unending until such time as you sell the animal or the animal perishes.

I have found and am convinced that a conservative approach to horse ownership is an intelligent course to follow. Hasty decisions made by an uninformed owner or buyer have a much more distinct possibility of producing an adverse effect, and in this situation, you are not the only one affected by the adverse outcome.

I truly see horse ownership and the purchase of a horse as an important and significant consumer transaction—a business decision. Therefore, we should approach the premise of purchase and ownership with as much information and caution as possible. As you will soon realize, there is much more involved in a horse purchase than simply writing a check and much more to ownership than buying a bag of feed and turning him out to pasture.

I will try to provide you (the reader and potential owner) with as much significant information as possible prior to and including the purchase as well as what to expect down the road. I would also encourage you to proceed even further with your research if you feel it is necessary. Far too many horse buyers make hasty and uninformed decisions due to the heat of the moment and emotion. This is human nature and not to be condemned, but I do stress a more researched and conservative approach.

Much of the advice that we receive is from other folks who have made mistakes in the past, and through their experience, they are attempting to alleviate the grief that you may invite. As you may suspect, people sometimes listen and sometimes they plead ignorance. But I can assure you that upon completion of this book, you will have a much stronger foundation on which to base your purchase and a basis to ask the hard questions that will determine your level of success.

You will see the word *professional* mentioned throughout the text of this book and its application to many different situations. Remember, you will be dealing with other people in this quest and may misjudge or misinterpret information related to you by others—including so-called *professionals*. This book will equip you with enough knowledge to ask the right questions and hopefully bring a favorable outcome.

Professionals in the equine business are generally or specifically involved in profit. They often earn their living training, instructing, breeding, boarding, or selling horses. Most professionals are honest, but some are not as ethical—just like any other business. Therefore, you should initiate all necessary steps to protect yourself from unscrupulous professionals by being knowledgeable and informed. It may even require you to adjust your own attitude to be effective in dealing with others. This is business.

While I respect and admire many equine professionals and sponsors, I discovered through my research and experience that the industry was so subjective that many of the things that I had been told turned out to be quite tainted and factually inaccurate. Unfortunately, misinformation can cause hard feelings in a business relationship and certainly affected me as a horse owner. While opinions are something to be considered, they can also provide erroneous or misleading information. As a result, new owners who are inexperienced or uninformed are often the victims of overzealous professionals.

You will also have an opportunity to examine your legal position and how it may affect you and your horse. Much to my dismay, state laws in most jurisdictions offer little protection for the consumer—specifically the equine owner—by unfairly shielding equine professionals and sponsors from liability exposure. While I totally understand the position of professionals concerning inherent liability, the industry could not thrive without owners like yourself. It has been my hope for several years that the interests of consumers in the equine business be better represented.

I am quite sure that you are considering your purchase based upon your admiration of horses and the relationship that will surely blossom between the both of you over the years to come. This is an irreplaceable and beautiful experience. So, it is very important that you not only participate in the industry but become an integral part of it. In other words, your personal, emotional, and financial involvement will positively influence the industry and applicable governmental bodies to better balance the scales between the consumer and professionals. This should be the goal of all horse owners.

It is my sincere hope that you benefit from reading this book as much as I benefited from writing it and that you will strive to make your relationship with your horse as gratifying as possible. If I have assisted you in any way, I consider this work to be a success and wish you all the good fortune in your future horse ownership experience.

Chapter One: The Commitment of Ownership

Owning a horse is a luxury that few individuals come to experience firsthand within their lifetime. Yet most people, young and old, have been intrigued at one time or another by the horse. Its grace and elegance are beheld in the hearts of all who have crossed paths with them. Certainly, much can be learned from them as we watch in wonderment and ponder their thoughts, movement, and fluid motion and how it relates to us and our place in the world.

All things tend to have a place in the world, and the horse is no different. Horses and human beings have interacted and coexisted with irrevocable success for generations. Their bond has been a partnership that has flourished through pleasure, work, and war and is likely to continue for generations to come.

Much can be said about horse ownership. Without question, the advantages are immense, as well as the enjoyment that a horse can bring to its owner. Horses, by nature, are accustomed to pleasing man/woman. He/she will try with great fruition to obey every command and to perform all requested maneuvers with precision if he/she believes that it will please you. This dedication is not often found amongst many other animals—or human beings for that matter. Therefore, understanding that the basic premise of the animal psyche will aid you in discovering if a horse will benefit you in some way.

It is essential that your horse has a prescribed function. Without function, there is no means to an end. In other words, the horse will be unable to please you or perform sufficiently without a mission in which to engage. Whereby, there exists no means to an end simply because you have not provided a beginning.

Many essential decisions are left for you to make concerning your proposed ownership. I would suggest great consideration before ever making a final decision to make a purchase. As with many amateurs, you have never purchased a horse, and there is certainly no disgrace in that. Everything is new at least once, and this is no different.

However, I would suggest developing a process or an agenda to ensure that you do everything possible, leading to the correct decision.

This book has been designed and written in a specific progression that I encourage you to follow—especially if you are a first-time buyer or a purchaser of little experience. I have attempted to make the purchase process as simple yet concise as possible so that you may enjoy the advantage of pre-existing knowledge. In this case, as with any other purchase, I think that you will find that the better informed you are as a consumer, the better chance you have of walking away satisfied with your performance as a buyer. Keep in mind that buying is as much an art as selling a product.

While I sincerely believe that the progression of information that I have proposed will be effective for you, I would also add that no particular methodology is carved in stone. Hopefully, as you become more seasoned as a buyer, you will enable yourself to make desired additions or deletions that better suit your style of thinking. The point is that establishing and perfecting an effective methodology will provide you with a strategy.

Your pre-purchase strategy is the skeletal framework by which all future decisions will be formulated. It is always helpful to have a plan in place of which you take adequate time to study and revise until you feel comfortable with the proposed progression. With a plan developed, you will find that your level of confidence will be invariably higher. In turn, it is likely that you will be more effective as a purchaser.

Research

Since this business and process are probably new to you, it would be advisable to get an education on the subject. I am a firm believer in familiarizing oneself with new projects. The equine industry is unique, and if you are totally new to the industry, there will be many aspects of it that you will likely not understand.

Researching the subject will be your first step in making a major decision that will likely affect much of the rest of your life. It is important to realize that with proper medical care and upkeep, your horse could live as long as 30 years or more. So, it is very important that you are thoroughly aware of the vital aspects of horse ownership such as life expectancy.

There are many consumer publications that are available to you through subscription or at your local library or retail bookstore that offer a plethora of information concerning the subject of horses and horse ownership. Publications such as *Equus, Horseplay, Practical Horsemen, Horse Show,* and *Horse Illustrated,* to name a few, closely follow issues concerning the horse industry and their owners. These consumer publications follow horse-related issues daily and can provide you with very intriguing and educational information that will surely be useful to you as a prospective buyer. You would be well-advised to obtain as many of these periodicals as possible and scan them for information that you feel relates to your situation. Some even periodically publish a cumulative index of past articles within prior issues, which is a very effective way to pinpoint specific articles that you may want to read over.

Another fine source of research information is your public library and the internet. There is no question that you will find many books written on a number of subjects within the central subject of the horse, but even more importantly, you are privy to congressional records pertinent to equine issues, a wide variety of newspaper articles that relate to the equine industry and databases full of inherent information.

Remember, your decision to purchase a horse not only has a lasting effect on you, but also affects another living, breathing entity. For that reason, you must institute logic and fairness into your thinking and reasoning processes. Lack of information due to poor or no research at all will have a lasting effect on both of you.

Talk to Others

Experts are another fine source of information that may assist you in making specific choices. The question is: what constitutes an *expert*? Unfortunately, there are many self-proclaimed experts in the equine industry, and it is painfully obvious (at least this has been my experience) that very little is required of an individual to be considered an expert. In my eyes, there are specific requirements that I have before I will consider that person to be an expert—and I have probably offended more than one person by questioning their expertise. However, this is the only way to keep the business honest and ethical. In subsequent chapters, we will attempt to define an *expert* and a *professional* and will consider them nearly one and the same for our purposes. For now, we are simply considering opinions.

There is no better way to learn about a particular subject than to engage in dialogue that pertains to that subject. A good source of information would be to speak to someone who has already taken the plunge into horse ownership so to speak. While this person, be it a friend or acquaintance, may not qualify as an expert in the field, you can at least draw a subjective viewpoint from that person. With this information, you will be able to form some initial impressions and opinions after hearing the viewpoint of another owner. It would be of some benefit if you could inquire about the commitment involved with their experience of ownership. You can be sure that levels of dedication will differ from person to person, but you are sure to hear an array of experiences that you should file for future reference. Absorb as much information as you possibly can through this process.

It is a distinct possibility that you may become somewhat frightened when you hear a horror story. Don't be alarmed, as there is probably another one that is worse. While bad experiences may make the person appear cynical, you should file that information for later use in the decision-making process. You must be aware that with the good points of ownership, there can be bad ones as well.

There's little mystery that some people become inherently more attached to an animal than another person. I am a person who becomes very attached, and I probably dedicate much more time than the average owner in some cases. I realized that my horse, Rhythm King, was not a human being, but I can assure you that he was a major part of this author's life and family. I would feel very comfortable stating that I spent more money on him than many folks spent on their children. Notwithstanding that fact, I cannot fault another person for not feeling the same emotional attachment that I may feel, although I may not necessarily agree. This is simply my opinion. And while it is only my opinion, my experience, as well as that of others, is worth listening to and drawing some conclusions from.

When you choose to exchange ideas and experiences with other people for your reference, remember that opinions are dominant in the equine industry. In fact, this is one of the most opinionated industries in existence from what I've seen. I have, in the past, entered many business enterprises and situations to match. I can attest to the fact that each company, whether large or small, had a system that was unique to all others. Each person that you talk to and each facility that you patronize, each breeder, barn manager, writer, and equine practitioner will all have differing opinions on a variety of subjects. This does not mean that any opinion is necessarily erroneous, but an opinion is an opinion, nonetheless.

Achieving Direction

Through your initial research, interviews, and conversations, you're attempting to achieve direction for yourself. You must make choices to satisfy your needs and desires and to facilitate your own abilities. There are numerous choices that are pertinent to your pre-purchase process. You will be responsible for choosing a specific breed of horse that may meet your needs. You will attempt to make choices concerning your desired events and usage and be required to evaluate your own physical abilities. One thing is for certain: if you are to make an intelligent purchase, you must be willing to provide the level of dedication and commitment necessary to maintain your horse's health, living conditions, training, and mental well-being. Without dedication and commitment, you will not be what I refer to as an *effective owner*.

An effective owner is one who provides all the functions on a continuing basis without reservation.

Horses are high-maintenance, and that can mean high-dollar at times. So, it is important to realize precisely what dedication entails. I can assure you that horse ownership is not always caramel apples and cotton candy, but I am convinced that the good far outweighs the bad and the challenge in that regard.

There are numerous breeds of horses that are suitable for any number of events and functions. Like dogs, for example, horse breeds have specific characteristics that are unique to that breed and characteristics that may make them suitable for certain prescribed purposes. Notwithstanding, do not impose too strict a limitation to breed, as you may not follow your intuition and heart. An intelligent choice of breed is important, but what you find appealing about that individual horse is equally significant to you as a buyer. For example, a Hanoverian is a fine dressage horse, but I happen to have used Rhythm King, a Polish Arabian for dressage, and he was quite impressive and a beautiful mover. A quarter horse is a fine prospect for racing but also makes a beautiful and dependable jumper. Furthermore,

Arabians are commonly used for endurance riding, as they are seemingly tireless, yet they are also used for racing. So, imposing strict limitations on breed is sometimes needless and can be premature. I would suggest that you carefully evaluate each breed that you are considering and even some that with which you are unfamiliar, thus inspiring objectivity in your choice. Some horses are not for all people, and that is important to realize.

Attempt to evaluate your choice of events and use. The terms: *dressage, stadium jumping, combined training, eventing, pleasure cutting, raining, hunting,* and *barrel racing* are all common to horse riding, but all are considerably different. It is essential that before you choose your horse, you should decide what events and uses are of interest to you and what events and uses are realistic. This will enable you to make a more informed decision based upon the animal's physical abilities and your own. Not all horses are suitable for certain events.

Obviously, if you desire a jumper, you must choose a horse that has the strength and agility to do so. Some horses do not have that innate ability. I attempt to stress that a buyer should realize that horses, such as people, have their own limitations. If you can recognize these limitations and their impact on performance, you will be a much more effective buyer.

Another major concern in seeking direction is a horse's temperament. Horses are all individuals and do have their own personalities and traits. But as I stated, certain breeds do seem to have somewhat universal behavioral characteristics. I think that we could agree that we would all like to own a very level-headed and consistent horse, but this is not always the scenario. Like humans, horses have bad days, and many things such as feed, environment, and weather all impact a horse's mood, performance, and temperament. They're just like us. They have good days and bad days.

If you are concerned with temperament, you may want to carefully examine your potential horse's pedigree. Breeding can and does have a tremendous effect on the type of personality that offspring possess. You would also be well-advised to carefully examine the sire and dam of your prospects if possible so that you may make an evaluation. If they are not on hand, try to contact the owners and ask some questions regarding habits and behavior. Most horse owners and breeders are very cooperative when it comes to helping a new owner.

I recall a trainer, who considered himself to be an expert, making a statement to me when I became a new owner. He said, "that horse won't love you, because they are too stupid to understand you." This was yet another opinion in a long line of less-than-expert advice. Believe me, there is nothing further from the truth. You may rest assured that the bond that can be developed between the two of you can be immeasurable if you are willing to invest the time. You will also come to find out that horses are anything *but* stupid. They do have some uncanny abilities. As you are sure to see in the future—should you ever become an owner—these abilities are for you to discover. Rest assured that they are some of the most wonderful aspects of ownership. Therefore, I could not bear revealing them to you.

Commitment and Dedication

To be an effective owner can no doubt be time consuming. It would be wise for you to consider how much time you are willing and able to spend with your potential new companion. To be quite honest, the literal amount of time that you spend with your horse will determine many factors. The most important aspect in consideration of available time is to make certain that you are completely honest with yourself. If you approach the time-element in this way, you are more likely to be successful in achieving a happy and healthy relationship with your horse.

Ideally, you should be willing to spend at least every other day with your horse within his environment if possible. Initially, hours should be spent grooming and handling so that he/she may become familiar with you, the sound of your voice, and your touch. You're attempting to establish a good rapport and sense of trust for the future between you and your horse. You will find that if the animal feels comfortable with you, he will be more likely to perform for you and put trust in your judgment. It is ironic that a 1,500-pound animal must be so trusting of the rider, but horses are not predatory and somewhat anxious given their size.

Owning a horse is sort of a marriage in a way. You will soon see that your horse will become part of your routine. Depending on the boarding arrangements that you will choose and the location of your horse's living quarters, you may be required to travel some distance to see him/her. You may be also responsible for his feeding and exercise which may consume some of your time.

Commitment and dedication are the operative terms here. It is true that you may board the horse in a facility referred to as a *full-service facility* and alleviate yourself from the responsibility of feeding, exercise, grooming, and training, but you will be sacrificing some of the opportunity to experience the horse's development—and your own. Although I used to board Rhythm King at full-service stabling facilities, I continued to visit him regularly and handle all the aforementioned duties if I was present to do so. I enjoyed it. To be fair, if your horse is boarded at a good full-service facility, they are getting food, pasture turnout, and other care and socialization that they enjoy if you are short on time. Naturally, this is what you pay for.

As much as I would like to dictate the terms of ownership to others at times, I would be remiss to do so. But I am not at all reluctant to make recommendations here so that you understand your choices. You must remember that horse ownership is a big responsibility, and I feel that to do it effectively, you should have the proper amount of time available. Unfortunately, the amount of time felt to be sufficient will differ from owner to owner. All in all, the best thing that we can hope for is that every single animal gets the necessary care and maintenance to sustain it through life. Anything more is icing on the cake.

My last point with regards to commitment and dedication pertains to the question as to whether a given person can take on the responsibility. If you are a parent reading this book, it is essential that if you are purchasing this horse primarily for your child that you understand the ramifications of your decision. While it may seem very gracious and generous to provide such a wonderful gift to your child, I have seen few children who handle the responsibility well. I in no way mean to denigrate your child or any young person reading this book, but very often, this gift becomes neglected because the young person becomes disinterested or chooses another hobby. In addition, many parents graciously provide the horse for the child in hopes that he or she will take care of their companion as often as prescribed. Unfortunately, this plan often backfires.

Thus, if you are a parent who plans to make the commitment to purchase the horse for your child, the best advice is to make plans to be involved yourself. If you were simply trying to find an activity for your child to keep them out of the house, I would suggest swimming or a trip to the mall. Do not punish a horse for you and your child's lack of dedication or level of responsibility. It's just not fair to the horse.

You must also take into consideration that there are specific business-related activities that must be attended to by an adult. I have seen numerous situations where a parent of a minor horse rider has left the entire process up to the child. A minor who has not yet reached the age of majority cannot legally sign insurance release forms, stable care arrangements, veterinary decisions, training, etc. These points should be attended to by an adult. You'll also probably find that no responsible barn manager would allow this situation to persist, but there does exist the possibility that an unprofessional proprietor may allow this irresponsible situation to occur. I can assure you that this is not within your child's best interest nor your own.

If you plan to be involved from afar, please educate yourself about the activity and the processes involving ownership. It is a great example to set for your child and one that they will hopefully emulate in the future. Often, the desired level of dedication and commitment is a tone set by the parents which makes for a great life lesson. Many stabling facilities are full of great people who all love horses and the activity. They all have the potential to make great mentors as well.

Financial Responsibility

To be direct and to the point, horses are a very costly enterprise, and it is best if you realize that fact from the outset. Oftentimes, the potential buyer is not cognizant of the fact that your monetary and time investment is ongoing for the entire duration of ownership until the horse dies or until he/she has been sold. You must be aware of the commitment that ownership demands.

Many purchases are simply made on a whim or by emotion. Every year, your local *Humane Society* and *SPCA* are inundated with patrons during the Christmas and Easter seasons. These patrons are searching for that cute cuddly face that will grace the household over that special holiday. All too often, though, many of those once cute and cuddly faces that were so graciously adopted the year before are now grown and do not represent the novelty that they once did within the home. Many of those now desolate faces are seen right back where they came from—abandoned in a shelter. And, yes, sometimes needlessly destroyed. This morbid means to an end is due wholly to the utter lack of responsibility and dedication of irresponsible owners. This fact truly hurts me—even as I write this passage—

but it is too often reality. For that reason, I advise you to take great care of making your future decision, because that horse depends on you.

If you are truly intent on being a horse owner, you must accept the financial responsibility and reality that accompanies ownership. And I would simply be lying if I said that a horse was inexpensive. Unless you are planning to keep the horse on your own property, you will be faced with a number of expenses that include, but are not limited to: stabling fees, farrier costs, veterinary fees, legal fees, insurance fees, equipment cost, proper apparel, safety equipment, tack, nutritional supplements, and other related costs. Believe me when I say that the cost of these items can be quite high, and many of the items are ongoing and on demand.

According to what part of the world you live in, you will be faced with those aforementioned costs. Location can have some bearing on the cost of a stable facility. For example, in the southeast where I reside, a very nice full-service facility may cost $800 or more per month. However, the same quality facility may cost $1200 and above in the northeast portion of the country. It is all subjective. Therefore, these costs are relative to purchase and should be researched prior to purchase. As will be discussed in Chapter 4, veterinary costs can also be quite costly, and you are always taking a gamble with relation to your horse's health.
Fortunately, equine insurance is available for your horse. And I wholeheartedly recommend it! If not, you are left with the full burden of payment, and it can be very expensive.

When I used the term *luxury* in the very first sentence of this book, I truly meant what I said—horse ownership is a luxury for most people and not for everyone. But that does not mean that you are excluded from enjoying the stimulation and satisfaction of horsemanship. There are many options and alternatives for ownership that can and should be considered, and we will discuss those options at length in upcoming chapters. Inasmuch as I will try to persuade you to purchase a horse, I will present you with information that may ultimately dissuade you from making that commitment. That's okay! In either case, I will consider my efforts a success. Keeping you from overcommitting or making a costly mistake is as noteworthy as helping you make your decision to purchase. Remember, your initial purchase will likely be the most inexpensive and least taxing part of future ownership.

Chapter Two: Leasing As an Option

Now that you have a clear understanding of the commitment and dedication involved with horse ownership, you may want to consider a leasing arrangement as an option to an actual purchase. A leasing arrangement can be very advantageous to you as an alternative to being a buyer, as it gives you the ability to get hands-on experience in dealing with a horse on a day-to-day basis without the commitment of a full-blown purchase. In this way, you may better see precisely what is involved with horse ownership and use a lease agreement as a trial run.

There is also another advantage to leasing that is converse to ownership—the ability to walk away from the horse with no responsibility for its care or expenses. Non-owners have many options that make regular use of a horse more affordable as opposed to the ongoing upkeep and maintenance that an owner will likely incur.

Leasing arrangements have no exact definition, and there are numerous types of leases that you may want to consider. I will describe some common leasing arrangements that are initiated along with their advantages and disadvantages so that you may weigh the option that best suits your needs.

First, the **Off-Season Lease**. This type of leasing arrangement is common with trail riding facilities, summer camps, and in areas where inclement weather does not allow for year-round use. Many facilities that have horses used in the previously listed venues find it very economical to locate the horse in a good home until next season rolls around. With this arrangement, you are expected to feed, exercise, provide farrier and veterinary services, and care for the horse in exchange for having use of the horse at no additional charge to you. The horse may be kept on your property or boarded in a stable facility. Both situations must be acceptable and approved by the horse owner, and it is common practice for the owner or their representative to check the facility that you intend to use.

In this situation, the owner attempts to place the horse with a caring, responsible family, or individual. In many cases, horses are purchased through these owners once the family has cared for the horse and grown attached to him/her. This is one of the finest situations for these types of horses, because they are sometimes sold to a caring family who may not have otherwise even encountered each other.

As a lessee, you enjoy several advantages: 1) You have a horse available for your use at any time. 2) You have a unique opportunity to try horse ownership without incurring a purchase. 3) You will have a chance to experience all the enjoyment along with the responsibilities that accompany caring for a horse. 4) This arrangement also gives the amateur equestrian a chance at full-blown ownership without the remittance of the initial purchase price.

Rest assured, however, although no money may change hands as part of this arrangement, you will incur the cost of bedding, food, farrier service, veterinary services if needed, hay, and all the necessary products for grooming and upkeep. If you are in custody of the horse during the winter months, you will also need to provide blankets. So, your arrangement is not without cost.

The off-season leasing arrangement gives you a very good opportunity to reap all the benefits of ownership without the initial investment. It also provides a horse with a much-needed change of scenery and the necessary companionship that makes horses thrive. But beware, you may become very attached to the horse. If you are human, a bond is likely to be established between you, the horse, and even your family when he leaves. It will be just like bidding farewell to a family member. It can be very difficult, and it often happens.

One horse leaves a very vivid impression on my mind. In fact, I personally bid him farewell as he returned to a camp in Brevard, North Carolina. Champ, as he was called, was a 36-year-old Clydesdale-cross that worked as a trail horse for many years. He probably taught more children about companionship than you and I put together. Champ annually traveled to South Carolina for the winter months where temperatures were more conducive to winter use. I watched Champ compete in what would likely be his last show. All the children that rode him so proudly that day were exhilarated by the many ribbons he wore on his bridle, and I could not help but think that this was what ownership was all about. Champ still moves well and is sound, but his eyesight was degenerating. Needless to say, he would have to retire. Without an off-season program, I would have been denied the privilege of watching and respecting such a gallant friend. I never saw Champ again, but I will always support this type of arrangement for the prospective owner or horse lover because of its benefits to the horse and the lessee.

The second type of lease is the **Riding Club Lease**. There are many facilities nationwide that provide horses for riders to use based upon membership fees. Often, members are entitled to the use of a horse on specific days as the schedule permits. With this type of lease, you pay a monthly maintenance fee as do all riders who utilize this arrangement. Those fees are used for routine expenditures related to the horse's care and housing.

These facilities often operate on a seasonal basis. This does not necessarily mean that the facility is closed part of the year, but it may mean that you will pay seasonal prices for usage of the horse. Therefore, if you belong to a club that is associated with fox hunting, for example, you'll likely pay more during the hunting season than you would pay otherwise. This is not unreasonable, but it should be understood.

The club of your choice usually owns all the equipment along with the horses. This will enable you to use their equipment instead of purchasing your own—which can offer substantial savings. If the cost of equipment is not a concern, you will probably be allowed to use your own if it meets the club's specifications. Always inform your club manager of any equipment changes that you may implement to avoid any misunderstanding or possible damage to the animal.

Fortunately, veterinary care and farrier costs are also absorbed by the facility with a riding club lease. These costs can sometimes be exorbitant to incur and are not your responsibility in this arrangement. I would strongly suggest purchasing an equine liability insurance policy at your cost, however, just in case you cause injury to the animal or another patron. We will discuss equine insurance at length in another chapter, and you will better understand my recommendation.

As in our last arrangement, you pay no initial purchase price for the horse, but you are somewhat limited in this type of lease. 1) You are only able to use and care for the horse on your prescribed day regardless of weather conditions or the horse's state of mind or soundness. 2) You also have no input with respect to decisions surrounding the maintenance of the horse. 3) You also have a few riders that will be using the horse when you are away. Also be aware that not all the riders using the horse will ride at the same skill level or have the same philosophy about training. 4) Lastly, some horses simply may not like being ridden by five different riders a week.

The advantages of this type of lease are: 1) You know exactly what your monthly cost will be for using your horse. 2) You are practically free of any responsibility and come walk away at any time. 3) You are comfortable that the club is taking proper care of the animal, and you may not establish a bond that might otherwise keep you from parting.

It is my opinion that a reputable facility will take your concerns into consideration should you share them with the stable manager since you have an interest in the horse. I would suggest thorough investigation of the club's reputation, management, facilities, equipment, and available records. Do not patronize an establishment that clearly has no interest in the feelings or well-being of their horses and only seem to be driven by profit. There is much to be said about the profit-motive in business, but when these animals sustain that enterprise, they deserve respect and proper care.

The third type of leasing arrangement that may fit your needs is a **Partial Lease**. This type of agreement involves you as a part-time owner without incurring all the costs common to full ownership. For example, you may be familiar with a person that owns a horse that interests you for the purposes of learning or honing your present skills. Additionally, you may know the owner is only capable of riding and caring for the animal three times a week. Of course, there are four more days in the week in which the horse is not used, groomed, or given companionship. This is an excellent opportunity for you to approach the owner and propose an arrangement that would give you use of the horse the other days he/she is available.

You and the owner can come to some agreement as to how often the horse should be used in each seven-day period. I believe that like any athlete, your horse *needs* time off from performing work. Therefore, approach any arrangement based upon a five-day work week. Don't forget how important the other two days of grooming, massage, or a cool bath can be for the horse.

The partial lease is essentially the sharing of boarding costs. However, it will appear that you are basically renting time with a horse for its use. Notwithstanding the interpretation, you will enjoy the advantages of at least part-time ownership.

Please be advised that this type of arrangement can be a bit tricky. You may become very attached to the horse, as I mentioned previously, or conflicts can sometimes arise because of this type of lease because you and the owner may not have specific plans for the horse concerning competitions or events. You must remember that the owner makes all decisions concerning the welfare and use of the horse, so it is essential that a specific list of conditions is established to avoid any conflicts that may cause hard feelings between the two of you. Remember, companionship and learning are the primary goals for you and the horse.

Before you enter this type of lease, ask the owner these questions: 1) What days will I be given to use the horse? 2) Is grooming and maintenance of the horse equally divided? 3) May I make or share training decisions? 4) Will I be given the first bid on the sale of the horse should you decide to sell? 5) If the horse is injured, will I be credited for loss of use? 6) May I transport the horse to a show with your permission in advance?

These are but a few considerations to ponder in this type of lease. Remember, everything is negotiable, and your partial lease may differ considerably from my outline. Whatever the arrangement, make sure that you and the owner have a crystal-clear understanding of the terms. In this case, you may also want to opt for a written agreement for your protection and that of the owner. That is always recommended. If the owner is reasonable, he or she will not take a request for a simple contract as an insult. I will be more specific in the coming pages as to written agreements.

The fourth type of lease is an **On-Premise Lease**. This carefully constructed agreement is much like ownership but conducted on the horse's premises. You are given sole use of the horse for virtually whatever purpose if that purpose is reasonable and agreed upon by the owner or facility management.

Let us say for the sake of discussion that you live within ten minutes of *ABC Stables*. You've gone to the facility on several occasions and find it to be a comfortable setting with nice facilities. During your trips, you grew especially fond of a particular horse on the premises. She is owned by the facility and is used occasionally for school rides and some rented trail outings. You may want to inquire with the barn manager about that particular horse and the possibility of an on-premise lease.

If the horse is available for such an arrangement. You will want to ask for the option of spending a few hours with the horse to investigate her ground manners, temperament, and general personality. I would also advise a trial run on the horse just to make sure that you like the horse's movement and attitude while she is under saddle. You should also question the barn manager as to his or her previous experience with the horse and possibly talk to a rider or two that has ridden the horse in the past. This will give you an idea as to what to expect from the horse to ensure your safety and training goals. These two things should always be your main concern. There is no use whatsoever in leasing a Level 4 dressage competitor if you have only ridden a pony at a friend's birthday party when you were eight years old. When and if you happen to feel comfortable with a particular horse, you are ready to take the next step in preparing and negotiating an on-premise lease. But be realistic.

This lease should be clearly prescribed with a written agreement between the two parties. Although you may not actually own the horse or must remit the initial purchase price, this will still be a big investment. Unfortunately, your return on your investment is limited in that you do not build any equity in the horse and do not own him outright. When you are finished with the contracted period. But with this agreement, you should have the option of taking the horse to competitions or other outings at the location of your choice, training the horse to meet your needs, and full care of the horse at your discretion (excluding vet and farrier work).

You do have a few responsibilities that you may not otherwise have with this type of lease. 1) You will be responsible for all care other than what I have excluded. 2) You will have to groom, bathe, care for minor abrasions, provide regular hoof maintenance, groom the mane and tail, trim the face, ears, bridle path, and so on. In other words, this horse is your responsibility. So do not let her or yourself down.

If you have chosen this lease, you will also pay a more premium price. 1) An on-premise lease may or may not include tack and equipment. 2) It probably does not include incidental supplies used for maintenance. 3) It likely does not include blankets and sweat sheets. 4) It probably does not include a trailer for transport but may have one for rent when needed. Whereby, you will be required to provide those things that are necessary for you to operate but excluded by the lease. As these are probabilities, remember everything is negotiable, and you may be granted more privileges contingent upon the lessor's conditions.

Your lease fee should include board, feed and hay, farrier costs, veterinary costs, full boarding services that are provided to all other clients, all applicable vaccinations, and any other service that is regularly rendered at the facility. Make certain that your agreement is written in contractual form and clearly defines and describes the benefits and services that you will receive in exchange for your paid fee. I am a firm advocate that legal matters should be left to attorneys, and this instance is no different. If a local equine attorney is available, it might not be a bad idea to have them review any proposed lease agreement.

You should review any contract-for-lease *off* the facility premises before signing. I would also strongly urge you to allow your attorney to review the document for any flaws or clauses that do not meet state statutes or protect your rights as a consumer. In this way, you will be sure to start off on the right foot with your new project. Just be certain that you do not rely on an implied lease or a verbal promise. While the manager or owner may be a fine individual and astute businessperson, they should understand your concerns and respect your wish to make certain that you are properly advised and protected. It benefits all involved.

The fifth and most costly lease is the **Off-Premise Lease**. This type of contractual agreement is the most complex of the previous arrangements, in that you will need to be certain that all aspects of the agreement have been reviewed, described, and understood by both parties to ensure that no conflict exists at the outset.

If you are seeking the true experience and realism of horse ownership, this is your chance to jump in headfirst. As a condition of this lease, you will be taking the horse off the premises and transporting him or her to your own property or a stable facility. You have entered into an agreement with the owner that states that you will provide full care and maintenance of the animal for the duration of the lease and will return him in good condition or possibly agree to purchase him if that is an option described within the lease contract.

You will be required to purchase all equipment that is necessary to care for the horse in a fashion that he is used to or better. You may even be able to negotiate use of tack if you do not have that equipment on hand or if the horse requires specialized equipment that you cannot readily supply. If you are not transporting him to a stable facility, you will have to provide food, bedding, blankets, hoof products, fly spray, shampoo, hoof tools, brushes, wraps, and any other therapeutic equipment that may become necessary.

As you may imagine, this is the costliest arrangement available to you aside from purchasing your own horse. In fact, this type of lease can theoretically cost more than actual ownership in some cases. Why? First, you will be paying a lease fee to the owner each month. Second, you will most likely pay a stabling fee unless you own adequate property and facilities at which to house the horse. Third, you will have to absorb the cost of all necessary maintenance products. Fourth, you will now be responsible for all farrier costs including trimming and shoes. Fifth, you will be responsible for veterinary costs related to the horse while in your care.

You should realize that veterinary costs can be very high at times. Most likely, the owner will want to be notified as soon as possible if the horse receives a life-threatening injury or illness while you are leasing. You should be certain that you are authorized to make at least minor decisions concerning the treatment of incidental or minor injury or illness. In this way, you will not be required to burden the owner with every scratch but will certainly advise him or her if anything untimely occurs. Full disclosure is always the best policy. Try your best to keep the owner informed—even if it is simply a monthly status report.

The off-premise lease is not without benefits. You are given a unique opportunity to have the horse of your choice in your care and possession and should stipulate as to what your intentions are regarding the horse's use. If you intend to participate in dressage, you will now have the unlimited opportunity to do just that at your own discretion. You will also learn some valuable lessons regarding horse management; the process is not as easy as it appears. Even one horse can be a handful. At the very least, you will likely be able to make a concrete decision as to whether this activity is for you—at least at the ownership level. Remember, this arrangement requires the most commitment, and you always have the option of backing off in degrees to utilizing the other types of leases described previously. It is not a poor reflection on you if you do not possess the dedication and commitment that we discussed in Chapter One. However, it would be contemptible to fool yourself into thinking that you were up to the task if you were, in fact, not. You not only hurt yourself, but you also compromise the horse as well.

Unfortunately, I have witnessed situations just as I have described. Even more unsatisfactory, I have witnessed owners who avoided the commitment necessary to see the horse thrive. I have personally known horses who were gentle, lovable, and had talent who were left for days and weeks on end without any contact. This treatment, in my eyes, is undesirable. The horse could be sold or leased or given to a good home, but when you propose that option to the owner, they say that they could not possibly live without the horse. Yet for the next month, you will never see the owner. This situation often occurs with young people. They often do not seem to conceptualize the responsibility involved with caring for a horse, nor do they often comprehend the financial commitment that you, as a parent, have taken upon yourself in providing them with a commodity that is so rare.

It is extremely important that you, as a parent, instill in your child that this horse is of great importance. You should feel very comfortable in laying out ground rules to be followed in order that the child realizes that the horse will be cared for properly and that you expect him or her to contribute time and energy to the project. Whether you lease or own, I suggest that you be willing to be directly involved. In this way, you will set the most important example of all. In all fairness, I have seen many dedicated young people who love nothing more than spending time with their horse. They should be applauded.

Lastly, let us discuss the **Trial Lease**. This type of lease may take the form of any of the previously mentioned lease agreements. In this arrangement, you will be leasing the horse on a trial basis and recognize that money may or may not change hands because of this agreement.

The trial lease is an arrangement that is common to pre-purchase and usually comprises a much shorter period than other leases. As I mentioned, you may choose to initiate an on-premise lease as your pre-purchase trial. You are trying to decide whether to purchase or pass. Therefore, use whatever leasing arrangement that you feel best fits your needs. If you feel that a weeklong trial lease will suffice for your purposes, so be it. You may feel that an off-premise arrangement would be best to suit your needs. Whatever the application, take the time that you feel is necessary.

I would add that it is common practice for an owner or facility to relinquish a horse for a trial lease at no charge in many cases. In other words, you are given an opportunity to have the horse temporarily for a predetermined length of time—maybe a week or two. You get the chance to ride him and spend an adequate amount of time with him to learn a bit about his personality traits, eating habits, vices, and so on. This is kind of a test drive so to speak.

You can now see that there are numerous options for you to consider when thinking about horse ownership or purchasing. Remember, options equal choices. It is very easy to make a hasty decision when we see something that excites us. The more informed about your decision, the happier you will be based upon research and not novelty or emotion.

In conclusion, you will ascertain through a well-planned lease exactly what financial burden you will be accepting if you choose to make a purchase. Do not overextend yourself on a horse. *Always* plan for the worst-case scenario so that you can formulate a working budget, including the new member of your family. I do hate to beat a dead horse (no pun intended) but if you are unable to meet the financial obligations surrounding your horse, you will likely devastate the rider and yourself because of poor planning. Conservative thinking in this regard will serve you well.

The horse has no comprehension, whatsoever, of the decisions that you will make concerning his or her welfare. He simply desires companionship, food, grazing, grooming, and the occasional treat. The security you give him will make him feel at ease. However, if an arrangement goes sour, the horse will suffer both mentally and physically. You must gain your horse's trust in your relationship and will absolutely have to earn it. So, make the best decision that you can based upon the most reliable information available. This will ultimately bring you the highest level of reward and success in your horse journey.

Chapter Three: Equine Insurance

In July of 1985, the *American Horse Council* commissioned a study of the horse industry, examining its macroeconomic impact on the United States economy. This study was initiated to reveal the horse industry's integral economic makeup and define what role the industry plays in affecting the Gross National Product (GNP). According to that study entitled, *"The Economic Impact of the US Horse Industry,"* horses accounted for 16% of the gross national product. It was noted that horse owners and breeders spent more than $13.2 billion per year developing and maintaining their stock. It was also revealed that another $3 billion was generated by spectator-related equine sports.

According to statistics provided by *Horses Only* in 2025, the annual contribution of the national equine industry to the U.S. economy increased to $122 billion, estimating that 1.74 million people are employed directly and indirectly by the horse industry. With an estimated horse population of 7.25 million, there are 1.6 million households who own horses in the U.S.

Total industry contribution of $122 billion is significant by any standard. Therefore, it may be easier for you to understand the significance of the equine insurance industry if you understand the industry as a whole. For example, if you were the president of, *We Protect Insurance Corporation,* and your primary focus of business was homeowners' insurance, your company goal would be to insure every home in America. The equine insurance companies are no different. Their goal is to insure every horse, stable facility, and horse show. $122 billion is enough motivation for any company, and you can rest assured that equine insurance companies will compete to insure every penny.

One of the key elements involved with proposed horse ownership is accepting the responsibility of liability surrounding your horse and being realistic enough to realize that equine activity is one of inherent danger. I am also confident that in your close review of the previous chapters, you realize the level of commitment and dedication that I have mentioned so often. I also pointed out that you must be willing to accept the financial responsibility that can and will be involved. Yet, few amateur equestrians realize the necessity of equine insurance. While insurance is optional, I strongly recommend it for the responsible owner as a requisite. Without the proper coverage in place, you leave yourself and your horse (your investment) at great risk.

Within this chapter, we will thoroughly discuss several types of equine insurance and the coverage that I feel may be necessary for you as an owner. I will also present you with some hypothetical situations that may inspire great thought and add caution to your list of priorities.
You should realize that your risks are as exigent as that of the professional. And as with all risks, there exists social responsibility not only to protect one's investment, but more importantly, another's well-being.

Each time you mount your horse, you potentially endanger the well-being of another rider or spectator and the property of others. If you have spent time around horses, I'm confident that you have come to realize their strength and periodic unpredictability. These qualities do not make them less than desirable, but they do warrant consideration and protective measures be taken on the part of the responsible owner. Keep in mind that equine insurance is not strictly limited to owners. I also mentioned the need for proper insurance to be in place during certain leasing arrangements. It is imperative to realize that simply because you do not own the horse, you may still be held responsible for its actions, and there is no rider that is beyond losing control of a 1,200-pound horse.

Many amateurs and professionals alike irresponsibly opt to avoid carrying proper insurance coverage---either for economic reasons or because they were grossly misinformed about the intrinsic importance of equine insurance. Usually, this misinformation transpires from an individual through hearsay and lacks credibility. Individuals that make such ludicrous claims or misgivings are bluntly wrong. If, in any circumstance, you are encouraged not to have the proper coverage in place, I would advise you to steer clear of that person's advice. Ironically, many of the people who say that equine insurance is a waste of valuable resources are the folks who are considered *professionals*.

As I mentioned, you will encounter many professionals while considering and making your purchase or lease arrangement. Unfortunately, no one has provided a conclusive definition of what a *professional* is supposed to signify in the horse business. In my view, most of the people who claim to be professionals are not. I will, to the best of my ability, attempt to provide a conciliatory definition of a "professional" in this book. You will need guidance in the future, so the ability to identify a knowledgeable professional will be helpful if not imperative.

The following text within this charter will serve as a usable guide to assist you in making the correct inquiries and, more importantly, give you an opportunity to have the right answers in mind before you start. You will also have a very good idea as to the various types of policies, their applications, and approximate costs.

In General

Equine insurance consists of six basic categories that you will have to consider individually: mortality, major medical, surgical, loss of use, liability, and property coverage. Each protects different aspects of horse ownership and equestrian activities. All six *may* be necessary and recommended contingent upon your situation and needs.

Without proper coverage in place, you may put you and your horse at considerable risk. If your horse is injured or becomes ill, medical costs can compile quite rapidly. If your horse suddenly dies or is lost due to theft, replacing him can be quite expensive. If your horse causes property damage or injuries to another person, you may be faced with defending yourself against litigation. Legal costs are always typically high, and you may be faced with decisions that might have otherwise been avoided had you taken the necessary and proper precautions from the moment that you took possession of the horse.

Whether you have decided to purchase or you are initiating a lease agreement, I recommend having an insurance binder in place before you take possession of the animal and before any money changes hands. You should contact your equine insurance agent and advise him or her that you intend to purchase or lease and desire coverage to be in place prior to the actual sale or lease agreement (if required). I would advise not deviating from this policy, because it protects you and your investment from the outset.

If you do not have the proper coverage in place or something untimely occurs after you have signed a bill of sale, you are responsible for the horse from that moment forward. Am I attempting to instill a sense of caution in you as a buyer? Yes!

An insurance binder is also applicable when you have chosen the option of financing your purchase or when a lease contract has been drawn and signed. In both cases, another party has a vested interest in the horse. In a financing arrangement, the seller or finance company may require that you name them as a co-beneficiary of a mortality policy. This is perfectly proper and not unlike your automobile lender requiring you to have comprehensive coverage in place for the duration of your finance agreement with a bank or financial institution. In a leasing arrangement, you may simply be trying to protect yourself in the case that something untimely occurs such as the horse is stolen while in your possession. In either case, it is essential to have coverage in place. In a co-beneficiary situation, contact your insurance broker and advise him or her that you are naming another person or organization as the co-beneficiary of said policy.

If a loss is experienced during a financing agreement, you're responsible for reimbursing the seller or finance organization for that portion of the contract that has not yet been satisfied. If there is a surplus of funds, you will receive the proceeds that are in excess. Conversely, if any deficiency or negative balance exists, you would then be responsible for reimbursement of the other party to make them whole.

It is important to note that once you have signed a finance agreement, you are then the legal owner with a lien against the animal or your signature (your personal credit line). At that time, you become responsible for all decisions concerning his medical treatment, maintenance and care. If you have met your contractual obligations of the sale or agreement, only you can dictate your methods of treatment or decisions.

Sellers or professionals often finance the sale of their own horses. While this can be convenient, you may run into a situation that can occur should the horse become ill or injured and require medical care. I have seen sellers who were insistent about the medical treatment that you should provide according to their directions even though you own the horse and are paying installments set forth in the agreement. This type of misconduct can cause hard feelings, and if you happen to board your horse at the seller's facility, this situation can make a good relationship turn sour in short order. Make sure that any agreement for financing is made in a fashion that you will enjoy elsewhere should you deem moving the horse necessary. In this way, you will preserve your rights and avoid unnecessary conflict.

Now that you have a general idea of the need and function of equine insurance, let's now define each category and its significance in your insurance portfolio. Again, consider all six individual components as a package if the situation warrants.

Types and Coverage

1. Mortality Insurance

- Covers the death of a horse due to accident, illness, or humane euthanasia.
- Often includes theft coverage.
- Payout is based on the horse's agreed value at the time of policy issuance.

2. Major Medical Insurance

- Covers veterinary expenses for illness or injury.
- Includes diagnostics, medications, hospitalization, and follow-up care.
- Typically has annual limits ($5,000–$15,000) and deductibles.

3. Surgical Insurance

- Specifically covers surgical procedures, often with separate limits from major medical.
- May include anesthesia, post-op care, and hospitalization.

4. Loss of Use Insurance

- Provides compensation if a horse becomes permanently unable to perform its intended use (e.g., racing, showing, breeding).
- Requires extensive documentation and veterinary evaluation.
- Often pays a percentage of the horse's insured value.

5. Liability Insurance

- Protects owners from legal claims if their horse causes injury or property damage.
- Includes personal equine liability and commercial liability (for trainers, stables, etc.).
- Coverage limits range from $300,000 to $1 million or more.

6. Property and Tack Insurance

- Covers barns, stables, trailers, and equipment like saddles and bridles.
- May include fire, theft, flood, and vandalism protection.

Mortality Insurance

Your horse is not necessarily worth what you did or did not pay for him. To most owners, their horse is part of their family and invaluable. Unfortunately, your horse can perish with little or no warning like any other companion animal. This loss can devastate an owner and her family and cause unending anguish and sorrow. Often, the best medicine for your broken heart is a new companion. Sure, it may not replace your first or favorite, but it may enable you to lend purpose to your life as an equestrian and to ease your heartfelt pain.

If you took the proper precautions while your previous horse thrived, you will be able to replace him in short order. You should have previously included livestock mortality coverage in your equine insurance portfolio. This coverage grants you reimbursement in the event that your horse dies or is lost by theft. This coverage is essentially life insurance for your horse.

Keep the word *investment* in mind.

From the time that your horse is born, he is learning daily. You painstakingly teach and drill him to attain maximum enjoyment and effectiveness of purpose. Hours, weeks, and months are spent nurturing and caring for him. In the event that he was lost to death or theft, would it not seem fair to be compensated for his achieved value?

While your mortality coverage is in place, keep your broker informed of your horse's development and accomplishments. Professional training makes your horse more valuable. The fact that he is a proficient jumper makes him more valuable. For each award he wins, he becomes more valuable. Contact your broker each time one of these goals is attained. You will have the opportunity to increase the value of the horse within your policy, and your coverage will increase accordingly. But be aware that your premium may also increase in relation to the increase in value. Then, should anything adverse occur, you will at least retain what you have worked so diligently to achieve.

You may have been the recipient of a horse that was given to you by a family member or friend as a gift. Some mortality policies are based upon the purchase price of the horse and make that amount the determining factor in the limit of your mortality coverage. But what if he was a gift and you paid nothing? Of course, it would be ridiculous to be told that *"we can only insure the horse for the purchase price"* by an insurance broker. However, I have been told just that in some conversations with brokers.

Your best bet is to have a **Certified Equine Appraiser** establish the value of the horse. This written appraisal should be done at your expense, and you should insist that your appraisal be considered to establish your horse's value versus the appraisal of an insurance company representative—unless you are satisfied with his or her appraisal. I do not particularly support **Agreed Value Mortality Coverage**, so be aware that it does exist.

Another legitimate concern of the owner is theft. Theft is a problem in all facets of life as well as the equine industry. I recommend as a deterrent that you post a sign near your horse's stall informing all that he is insured. Your broker's name should be clearly displayed along with your policy number. This simple practice will serve as a deterrent to thieves. When you insure your horse, you create a paper trail. This makes your horse very unattractive to a thief. Your broker also has a vested interest in the horse and will provide you with assistance in the event of theft. He may also have a brochure available from the underwriter giving you advice in theft prevention. Naturally, with the advent of wireless video cameras, GPS tracking, and ID chip implants, stealing a horse is much more complicated than in the past and much less desirable to thieves.

In the event that your horse is lost by theft or some other means and your claim is paid, the subsequent recovery of the animal usually entitles the insurance carrier to take title and possession of the horse. So be prepared to reimburse the carrier for the paid claim in the event that the horse is recovered. I recommend that you exhaust all means of locating the horse before you ever accept payment from the insurance company.

Mortality coverage will provide you with a viable alternative to becoming totally inactive in the event of the aforementioned circumstances. The cost of this type of coverage is very reasonable as well. In my opinion, mortality coverage is essential and an intelligent choice. This coverage is your vehicle to recovery if you lose your horse to an unfortunate incident or he passes away. In either case, make this type of coverage part of your equine insurance portfolio.

<u>Major Medical Insurance</u>

Horses are similar to humans, in that, they are susceptible to illness and injury that may require professional medical treatment by a reputable equine practitioner. Many individuals purchase a horse without even considering the likelihood that sickness and injury are generally inescapable. It would then seem prudent that a preventative be in place from the outset to ensure that your investment and loyal companion can be properly cared for in a fashion that you would prefer for yourself.

Medical and surgical coverage will facilitate the unexpected expense and inopportune medical problems that your horse may experience. While it is certain that your horse will likely experience small difficulties here and there, remember that your horse is an athlete. All athletes must be cared for in a fashion that would allow them to continue performing, so maintenance is ongoing.

This type of coverage reimburses the reasonable and customary charges of a licensed veterinarian necessitated by illness, accident, or injury which occurs within the period that the coverage is in force. Medical and surgical coverage is available in different aggregate limits with applicable deductibles similar to other common types of policies other than those related to equine activity. You can choose the annual limits and varying deductibles at your discretion that meet your needs and financial situation.

The cost of treating serious injury, illness, or disease can be quite costly. Without this coverage in place, you may be left with less-than-desirable options should you not have the resources to pay out of pocket. Options such as destroying the horse are needless when you consider that the cost of insurance coverage is reasonable and available. There is little excuse to be forced to destroy your horse due to a lack of responsibility on your part.

In researching the policy, make sure that you are aware of any **exclusions** that may apply to your policy. These are specific conditions not covered that the underwriter excludes within the text and conditions of the policy. Examples of common exclusions are animals used for racing purposes, cosmetic surgery, castration, and postmortems. These exclusions are designed to protect the underwriter of the policy. Therefore, study policy wording carefully. If you have any questions regarding the text of the policy, consult your insurance broker. If he or she is unable to answer questions to your satisfaction, do not hesitate to contact the issuer of the policy for clarification of the terms. Exclusions are generally not unreasonable.

It is imperative that you have medical and surgical coverage as injury and illness are probable at some point. Realistically, we cannot expect that a horse will be totally free of any physical difficulties or illness. Your horse's health will likely be influenced by many factors, and the degree of problems that may occur will differ with each horse. The activity in which you participate may also have a direct influence on the types of problems that may occur. For example, dressage horses commonly suffer from a condition called *bog spavin*. This condition occurs in many cases due to the great demand put on the horse's rear end. It is a common problem and will likely require a treatment regimen at some time—which can be quite costly.

Sadly, I have seen many horses who required medical treatment and did not receive it as needed. The situation saddens me due to the fact that the owner was not astute enough to provide proper protection for the horse knowing that physical ailments would likely arise at some time in the future. I have often heard excuses such as cost, economic reasons, or *"I didn't pay that much for the horse."* These excuses are inadequate in my opinion. Worst of all, the horse suffers while being an innocent victim.

It is also customary that a preliminary medical examination be performed on the horse by an equine practitioner to qualify your animal for coverage. Be certain that you do not make *any* false representations concerning his health or preexisting conditions. This could be construed as fraud and could later nullify your policy.

Surgical Insurance

Equine surgical insurance is a specialized form of coverage designed to protect horse owners from the high costs associated with emergency or medically necessary surgical procedures. Unlike general veterinary major medical insurance, surgical policies focus specifically on operations that require anesthesia and a licensed veterinary surgeon. This type of insurance is particularly valuable for owners of performance horses, breeding stock, or any equine with significant monetary or emotional value.

Typical coverage includes emergency surgeries resulting from accidents or acute illness, such as colic surgery or fracture repair. It may also extend to elective procedures if they are deemed medically necessary, including joint arthroscopy or tumor removal. Most policies cover anesthesia, operating room fees, and post-operative care, which can include hospitalization, medications, and follow-up diagnostics. Coverage is generally triggered when a procedure is performed under general anesthesia by a licensed veterinarian, though some policies may include limited benefits for standing surgeries performed without full sedation.

Equine surgical insurance is often offered as an add-on to mortality insurance, meaning the horse's life must be insured to qualify. Coverage limits typically range from $5,000 to $10,000 per incident with annual caps and deductibles that usually fall between $250 and $500. Some insurers offer co-pay options where the owner pays a percentage of the total bill—such as 20%—in exchange for lower premiums. It's important to review policy details carefully, as exclusions may apply to surgeries related to pre-existing conditions, congenital defects, or procedures performed outside of licensed veterinary hospitals.

The financial impact of equine surgery can be substantial. Colic surgery, for example, often costs between $7,000 and $12,000, while fracture repair can range from $5,000 to $15,000. Joint surgeries may fall between $3,000 and $8,000. Without insurance, these costs can be devastating, especially for owners who rely on their horses for competition, breeding, or companionship. Surgical coverage provides peace of mind and financial protection allowing owners to make medical decisions based on the horse's needs rather than the cost.

When selecting equine surgical insurance, owners should consider the horse's age, breed, and intended use—whether for sport, breeding, or pleasure. It's also important to evaluate coverage limits, deductibles, and any network requirements, such as treatment at approved veterinary facilities. Bundling surgical insurance with major medical or mortality coverage can offer broader protection and streamline claims.

Ultimately, equine surgical insurance is a smart investment for those owners who want to safeguard both their horse's health and their own financial stability. Whether the horse is a show jumper, trail companion, or breeding stallion, this coverage ensures that lifesaving procedures won't become a financial burden. For many owners, it's not just about protecting an asset—it's about honoring a bond between them and a loyal family member.

Loss of Use Coverage

Loss of Use insurance is a specialized form of equine insurance coverage designed to protect horse owners when a horse becomes permanently unable to perform its intended function due to unforeseen illness or injury. Unlike mortality insurance, which compensates an owner for the death of a horse, Loss of Use provides financial reimbursement when the horse survives but can no longer fulfill its designated role—whether that's competition, breeding, or work.

This type of policy is commonly used for high-value performance horses, such as show jumpers, dressage mounts, racehorses, or breeding stallions and mares. Coverage is triggered when a horse suffers a condition or injury that renders it permanently incapable of performing its insured use, and that condition is verified by a licensed veterinarian. The horse must be retired from its original discipline, though it may still be suitable for other purposes, such as pleasure riding or pasture companionship.

Loss of Use policies typically pay a percentage of the horse's insured value—often between 50% and 60%. For example, if a horse is insured for $100,000 and declared a total loss for its intended use, the owner may receive $50,000 to $60,000 in compensation. Some policies offer full-value reimbursement, but these policies tend to bring higher premiums and stricter eligibility requirements.

To qualify for a payout, insurers usually require extensive documentation, including veterinary reports, diagnostic imaging, and proof that the horse has been withdrawn from competition or breeding registries. In some cases, the insurer may retain ownership of the horse or require that it be marked or branded to prevent future resale as a performance animal. These stipulations are designed to protect the integrity of the policy and prevent fraud.

Loss of Use coverage often comes with exclusions. Pre-existing conditions, congenital defects, and injuries sustained before the policy was active are typically not covered. Additionally, temporary injuries or conditions that may improve over time do not qualify. Policies may also exclude certain disciplines or breeds, depending on the insurer's risk assessment.

When selecting Loss of Use insurance, horse owners should consider the horse's age, discipline, and value, as well as the financial impact of losing its utility. This coverage is particularly valuable for professionals whose income depends on a horse's performance or breeding potential. It provides a safety net that allows owners to recover part of their investment and make informed decisions about the horse's future care and use.

Ultimately, Loss of Use insurance reflects the reality that not all equine losses are fatal—but they can still be financially and emotionally significant. For owners who rely on their horses for livelihood, competition, or legacy, this coverage offers peace of mind and a measure of protection against the unpredictable nature of equine health.

While this type of coverage may not meet your needs or be necessary for your level of horse ownership, this option exists if needed.

Equine Liability Insurance

By far, the most essential element in your equine insurance portfolio is liability coverage. Owning a home, car, or boat involves certain risks. Owning a horse is no different. The fact is that equine activity has been referred to as one of the most dangerous sports in which one may be involved. This not only entails danger to you but danger to others as well.

There is much misinformation within the equine community concerning equine liability insurance. Much to my amazement, I have *never* personally heard one horse or barn owner suggest owning this type of coverage. Maybe I do not know enough people, but this fact is especially alarming and should raise serious concerns in the minds of socially responsible owners. *Socially responsible* refers to the owner that has a clear understanding of the damage that their horse may cause to person and property and has the aptitude to protect not only himself but those around him. Notwithstanding the circumstances, if your horse is responsible for damage to property or injury to a person, you may be held legally responsible and subject to litigation.

Many barn proprietors have been officially instructed by the state in which they operate to post signs of certain size specification advising equestrians that there is *"inherent danger"* in equine activity. It also goes on to state that an equine sponsor may not be held liable for injury or death to a participant. Rest assured that if your state has such a law guaranteeing immunity to an equine sponsor, it can most definitely be challenged by competent legal counsel. The reverse would also apply if you made a negligent mistake. In the case of property damage, just realize that your horse may kick a car door, break a barn door, damage a veterinary facility, or escape into the roadway and cause an accident. These things can and do happen to folks just like you.

Here is an example of an equine liability immunity law. Signs are to be posted at the facility to warn spectators and participants. In fact, failure to post the signs revokes the sponsor's protection set forth by the law:

"WARNING: Under South Carolina law, an equine activity sponsor or equine professional is not liable for an injury to or the death of a participant in an equine activity resulting from an inherent risk of equine activity, pursuant to Chapter 9 of Title 47 of the Code of Laws of South Carolina."

With proper liability coverage in place, the responsibility for damages, injury, or negligence rests with your equine insurance carrier who has indemnified you. Most insurers suggest a minimum of no less than $300,000 up to $1 million in liability coverage, but most often suggest the median of $500,000 in coverage. There is undeniable value in liability insurance.

If you are a homeowner, consult your homeowner's policy broker for inclusion of equine activity in relation to the liability coverage on your policy. If you rent property and carry renter insurance, you will want to do the same. I suggest putting all questions in writing before calling and taking notes of your carrier's responses along with the representative's name, date, and time. Retain these for your records to be safe. At times, your homeowner's insurance company may answer. Be prepared for somewhat vague answers from your carrier stating that *"you may be covered depending on the situation."* This is not the ambiguity we are seeking.

One of the most effective means of obtaining proper liability coverage in any given situation is the purchase of a **Personal Liability Umbrella Policy (PLUP)**. This type of policy is purchased independently of your home and auto insurance policies. If an action is brought against you, your homeowners or automobile liability portion will cover you to its imposed limit. However, if a plaintiff is awarded a settlement that exceeds those imposed limits, the (PLUP) would then kick in to cover the deficiency. Carriers of this type of policy will require you to have a minimum level of coverage in place with all other policies before you may purchase the (PLUP). If you do have this type of policy in place, make certain that it covers equine related activity.

Again, it is essential that you have liability insurance in place—preferably before taking possession of your new horse. Do not take anyone's word as to whether you can be held liable for the actions of you and your horse while involved in equine activity. The short answer is that you can definitely be held liable even when you are not necessarily at fault. While it would be incumbent upon a plaintiff to prove your negligence, you are still put in the position of defending yourself. It is also important to realize that given the inherent danger of equine activity, another party litigating against you is not necessarily personal in nature, but rather a reaction to circumstances that can and do occur. The reality is that carrying this type of coverage is the responsible approach for all parties involved. Remember, liability coverage is for your protection.

Choosing An Insurance Broker

Choosing an insurance broker is a very important but relatively simple task. First, interview several brokers and make sure that you are comfortable with him or her. You will be required to communicate with them on a fairly regular basis, so comfort is important. Second, ask for references that you will take the time to verify. Unless you verify your sources, they are typically less effective. Third, choose a broker that is in close proximity (if possible) so that you may consult them face to face as often as needed. Admittedly, this can sometimes be difficult, but it may be possible. The most effective means of communication is a voice matched with a face, but with today's internet convenience, you may find yourself completing this entire task online—which is perfectly acceptable. Fourth, research the prospective company through your state commissioner of insurance website to verify that this company is licensed to do business in your state and that no formal complaints have been lodged against them. Fifth, consult such publications as the *A.M. Best Guide to Insurance* for more detailed information concerning the company's financial status and assets. Lastly, compare information with a couple of companies to see which best suits your needs and the needs of your horse.

Once you understand the coverage available to you, take adequate time to review your options and evaluate your position. This will give you an opportunity to think with a clear head and avoid any undue sales pressure. In most cases, a good reputation and positive references, along with your own independent research, will serve as a guidepost to making the best decision.

Responsibilities of Others

Obtaining proper insurance coverage is a precautionary measure taken by a responsible owner. You have now taken the necessary and proper steps to protect your interests and those of your peers around you. The question is, have others around you been equally responsible?

If you are choosing a stable facility at which to board your horse, you should make legitimate inquiries prior to signing any stable agreement. You should assess the level of responsibility taken by the facility owners, instructors, trainers, and farriers on staff— all of whom should have the proper insurance coverage in place. Inquire whether they have a comprehensive **Errors and Omissions Policy (E&O)** in place. This type of professional liability insurance should be in place to protect these professionals in cases involving improper training techniques, misjudgments in horse care or shoeing, breach of contract, injuries, unsafe instruction, medical oversight, and other issues. Surprisingly, many professionals do not carry this important coverage. Please note that E&O does *not* cover bodily injury or property damage—that's handled by General Liability or Care, Custody, and Control (CCC) policies according to *Markel Group, Inc.* a global specialty insurance and investment holding company specializing in equine related insurance.

Unfortunately, asking a simple question about a professional's insurance coverage can be easily misconstrued, but a true professional will always be understanding of your concerns and will attempt to provide you with clear and concise answers. If you are given vague or evasive answers that would warrant great concern on your part as to you and your horse's well-being, you may want to consider another facility, trainer, or practitioner.

Chapter Four: Choosing Your Equine Practitioner and Farrier

 It has been said that the first three things that you look for when moving to a new town are a doctor, mechanic, and lawyer. If you are a horse owner, you will make one very important addition to that list of professionals—an equine practitioner. Your equine practitioner is a Doctor of Veterinary Medicine with a specialization in equine science and treatment. There is no other issue that supersedes your horse's health. Without a healthy horse, you will be unable to enjoy that special bond that you have established, and your horse will be unable to perform to your expectations or those of his own. For that reason, it is imperative that you thoroughly consider his health before you ever take him on as your own.

Equine practitioners are not as prevalent in the veterinary medicine discipline as one might desire. According to the American Association of Equine Practitioners (AAEP), there are approximately 6,500 licensed equine practitioners practicing in the United States. That's not many considering the estimated horse population of around 7 million horses. According to *DVM360* the number of equine veterinarian applicants is decreasing despite rising demand in 2025, citing *"debt, burnout, long hours, and work-life balance"* as the primary causes.

Notwithstanding those statistics, it is extremely important to connect yourself with a qualified equine practitioner. And it is beneficial to consider your choice with the same scrutiny that you would employ in choosing a physician for yourself. They are extremely important in your horse's life.

The Interview

One of the most effective ways to choose an equine practitioner is through the process of interviews. Once you have established an actual list of equine practitioners that you've compiled through recommendations, browsing the internet, and casual conversations with other horse owners, you should prepare a potential interview scenario to follow. Call ahead and set an appointment time and make clear that your intentions are to ask some general questions concerning all aspects of a possible vet/client relationship. It is beneficial to have some data on hand regarding your potential or current horse so that you may direct some of your questions to a subject with which you are familiar.

There is absolutely no substitute for a face-to-face conversation with someone who may play such an integral part in your life and that of your horse. You enable yourself to see precisely what rapport that you will come to expect in future veterinary interactions. You may even be a spectator while your prospective veterinarian treats another horse. In this way, you will see firsthand with whom you will be dealing.

Ask for a tour of the facility and premises if possible. Have the veterinarian explain the function of the equipment available for patients. If a surgical area is housed within the facility, the vet may invite you to have a look. One day your horse may be admitted for a surgical procedure, and it is much to your benefit.

During your tour, keep in mind that it is more of an inspection than anything else. While you may not be familiar with some of the sophisticated technology within the clinic or the advanced machinery used to treat the patients, you are certainly more than qualified to inspect the cleanliness and appearance of the facility—and there are some very impressive facilities out there. Ask to view the recovery room. This room is used after surgery for the purpose of recuperation following a procedure. You may find that most of the room is padded. This extra padding is in place so that the horse may not injure himself should he become disoriented after being anesthetized.

An equine veterinary clinic will likely also have boarding facilities used for recuperating horses. Check to make sure that adequate fresh water is provided and see that the water or bucket is free of contaminants. Inspect the condition of the food, bedding, contents within the stall and general cleanliness of the boarding facility within the clinic. Also, look at other animals recuperating on the premises and ask questions about their problems and conditions. You'll quickly become familiar with what equine practitioners and staff do on a daily basis.

Once you have toured the facility and feel comfortable with the cleanliness and appearance, have a dialogue with the veterinarian. Ask about his or her credentials and the credentials of any other practitioner or technician within the office, how long he or she has been in practice, any honors that he or she may have received, any clinical residencies that he or she may have done, and any specialized studies of or research to the veterinarian's credit. This will give you some insight into your prospective veterinarian's training and accomplishments which are important to you as a client and your beloved horse as a patient.

Lastly, ask questions that are pertinent to your situation and to your horse. Inquire about the cost of common procedures, common issues for your horse's particular breed, issues of concern in your specific geographical area, immunizations, feeding and supplement recommendations, and issues of concern for your intended use.

I have met some fantastic equine practitioners in the past who were great people and offered a wealth of information for those interested enough to ask. These medical professionals are very highly trained and do it because they love it.

The Veterinary Business

In 2023, according to *PW Consulting*, 68% of clients said they would travel over 50 miles for a board-certified equine surgeon. Practices offering specialized services (e.g., sports medicine, dentistry) saw 22% higher retention. Emergency care access was a major factor in provider selection. In 2025, *American Horse Publications (AHP) Equine Industry Survey (Sponsored by Zoetis),* surveyed U.S. horse owners aged 18+ who manage at least one horse. Top client concerns included: horse health and veterinary access, cost of horse keeping, and availability of specialized equine services.

It is important to establish a standard of care that *you* find acceptable for your horse, and it is possible that your standards may not match those of your stable neighbor. Suffice it to say, friendships can be strained because of imposed or implied standards of care that you may or may not find reasonable. Where I may choose to spend $2500 on a procedure, you may find it more than feasible to destroy the animal. This premise of feasibility may be due to your financial position. This is important to consider in the pre-purchase stage. In other words, you must be prepared to take on the financial burden if you are a responsible owner. As crass as it may sound, do not buy a horse if you cannot afford to incur the costs. This is just a harsh reality of which you should be aware.

If you have decided that you will give your horse all the care necessary to sustain him or her, you should be concerned about the cost. There is little question that the difficult part of your relationship with your equine practitioner is paying the bills. Hopefully you were very attentive to Chapter Three and have considered establishing a protective equine insurance portfolio which will alleviate much of the burden. With the proper coverage in place, you will find that your reparation will pay tenfold if something unfortunate occurs. As I also pointed out, your cost of coverage will seem like pocket change in the event that your insurance carrier foots the bill for major surgery.

Please keep in mind that your equine practitioner is also a businessperson; they must be. After all the clients have been serviced for the day, your veterinarian must calculate revenues and expenditures just like any other enterprise. If the veterinarian is in practice for him or herself, they have many fiscal responsibilities, but I am confident that most practitioners are reasonable when it comes to cost of treatment and charge accordingly. There is a lot to be said about the *profit motive* in business. Keep in mind that if your veterinarian is driven to succeed financially, as well as professionally, he or she will strive to perform at their best. On the other hand, veterinarians do what they do because they love animals. These folks have a gift that is quite unique to human beings. They are healers, and it seems that they are often capable of performing miracles.

Strangely enough, an office visit for one of my dogs is usually more expensive than a farm call for a horse, but procedures on a horse can obviously be costly. According to *The Pricer,* a veterinary farm call can range between $100-$200 per visit depending on location, time of day, and whether it is an emergency or non-emergency call. They also state that $100-$150 is the common range for standard weekday visits and $175-$250+ for emergency or after-hours calls—especially on nights, weekends, or holidays. Some practices charge $150-200 per hour if the visit includes multiple horses or procedures. Typically included are travel time and mileage, veterinarian time on-site, basic equipment and setup—although a separate exam fee may be charged at $50-$100 per horse. Some equine practitioners may offer you the opportunity to establish a billing account with their office, so be sure to inquire about payment options and conditions.

I do have some personal feelings with regards to veterinarians and their business that are worth sharing.

My goddaughter, Giovanna, is currently a second-year veterinary medicine student at Mississippi State University CVM. She earned a B.S. degree in biochemistry and took a gap year working at a veterinary hospital while applying to veterinary school. For those of you who may not know, admittance into a veterinary medicine program is exceptionally difficult due to the limited number of schools that offer the graduate discipline and the limited number of slots available within the programs. These programs are highly competitive. Also noteworthy is the fact that application fees to veterinary programs can run $1000 per application for prospective students.

The fact is that she would have had a far easier time being accepted into a human medical doctor's program and would have likely had multiple choices of schools. It is also noteworthy to mention the level of debt that these future professionals take on to enter the discipline. In her case, the debt load will be some $300,000 or more before she ever treats a patient and is compensated. Just like human medicine, the training regimen for veterinarians is highly demanding, and the work ethic required to complete medical school and work in the field exceeds what most people are capable of. Moreover, even general veterinarians are trained in multiple disciplines covering multiple species of animals. So, when I hear people complain about treatment fees, visits, and surgical costs, it is important to understand that these precursors are indicative of why their services can be costly. In Giovanna's case, she has made it very clear to me that her motivation is not money, but rather her love of animals. I know this to be true. So, keep in mind the sacrifice that these medical professionals make in order to provide the best care to your horse, livestock, and small animals.

Experience

Since we have considered credentials, reputation and cost, it would probably serve us well to consider experience. There is no mystery that experience counts highly on the performance scale for equine practitioners, and there is little doubt that a more seasoned professional can often provide a higher rate of success due to their prior history. But it is also important that younger and more inexperienced veterinarians be given an opportunity to develop their own history and experience. These are the folks that will be there when the others retire. It is quite easy to be fooled by youth or by a recent diploma on the wall. Ideally, we would all like to have the best of both worlds, but that approach may be unrealistic. Try to be objective about new veterinarians. You may be pleasantly surprised at the results of your open mind.

That thought leads me to another facet of choosing your equine practitioner and defining a professional. Your veterinarian has completed a postgraduate education and has also been exposed to hundreds of hours of practical experience. That person obtained credentials that identify him or her as an expert in their field. They are also required to certify with their state's regulatory board so that they may practice in that particular jurisdiction. Therefore, they have earned the right to be referred to as a doctor and have the evidence of authority to justify their title. These folks are trained professionals that have met the necessary regulatory requirements to obtain their title as an expert. As a potential purchaser, this professional is one whom you should consult and trust for accurate and objective advice.

By the same token, remember that much of what you will be told by an expert, such as your equine practitioner, is based upon their professional opinion. Although your veterinarian will base his or her analysis on factual information and scientific data, the methods of treatment from one veterinarian to another may differ. This occurs primarily because of a difference of opinion. What I am suggesting is a realization that getting a second and maybe even a third opinion is perfectly acceptable. My correlation between opinion and the professional is that a true professional welcomes you to seek a second opinion to justify or nullify his or her case in point. Moreover, most professionals will invite you to obtain a second opinion—especially in serious cases.

I can readily attest to the fact that since there are very few certified professionals that hold actual credentials, many of the folks involved in the equine industry are what I would refer to as *self-proclaimed* experts. I recall many instances when I was given advice that should have only been issued by a true expert holding the proper credentials and expertise. You should be aware that listening to too many opinions from those who are not properly qualified can lead to adverse results. Experience does matter in this business, but I would advise you to consult only a certified professional for medical diagnosis.

Communication

There is no more important aspect of a business-client relationship than the aspect of communication. I might even choose to refer to it as the art of communication. Without a clear and unobstructed line of communication, you may be left with many unanswered questions, a sense of doubt, and an uncomfortable state of mind. When choosing your equine practitioner, his or her ability to convey pertinent information to you as a concerned owner will likely determine whether you will ultimately choose that person to treat your horse in the future.

Expectedly, much of the language that will be used when diagnosing and issuing a treatment regimen will be totally foreign to you. Therefore, you will need to employ a practitioner who will take the adequate time to thoroughly explain any applicable point or terminology that you may not understand. I also suggest that you familiarize yourself with as much veterinary information as you can absorb. It is clear that if your equine practitioner was not qualified, they would not be practicing. But you may feel more confident if you are familiar with the existing situation through your own research.

It is to your advantage to request full disclosure of all anticipated charges that may be incurred in any given situation. I would find it unlikely that any equine practitioner would purposely attempt to deceive you with regards to treatment cost. However, when you have made clear that you want to be informed of any potential cost, you leave no doubt as to your position. The easiest way to obtain full disclosure of potential costs is to simply ask. Be direct and to the point, and you will establish mutual respect between you and your practitioner.

Lastly, your veterinarian's ability to keep punctual appointments, return calls or texts, and keep open lines of communication should lend weight to your decision. It is sometimes difficult to make plans around unspecific appointment times, but there are professionals who operate on a first come, first serve basis. If you are calling without an appointment and are attempting to have the clinic fit you into the schedule, exercise patience. Veterinary medicine is not an exact science, and other patients are also important. You would expect the same courtesy.

There is no doubt that communications can and do break down periodically, as we are all human and make mistakes, but without proper channels of communication between you and your equine practitioner, you are likely going to be unhappy from the outset. Not all people are meant to have a relationship, whether personal or professional, so it is important that you find your personalities compatible. If you are fortunate enough to find someone whom you can trust and feel comfortable with, then you have accomplished a major task associated with horse ownership. Communication is of the utmost importance, and you are sure to find that out in the future.

<u>Investigate</u>

First, I would suggest going online and accessing your county clerk of court online court records. This will give you the ability to access current and past court record information and to review any relevant lawsuits filed against a practitioner and the results of said legal action.

Second, consult your state veterinary medicine regulatory board to review any complaints or disciplinary actions initiated against the veterinarian. If the practitioner previously practiced in another state, you may also want to make certain to contact that prior regulatory board for public information.

Third, be aware that your potential equine practitioner will carry malpractice insurance, and your state regulatory body has most likely implemented coverage minimums that have been mandated by that particular jurisdiction regarding the state minimum amount of malpractice insurance that practitioners must maintain. Each state may be different, so you may need to clarify that information.

The Right Foot Forward

It is not difficult to imagine that a horse and his ability to perform is based upon four very important mechanisms—his feet. So, you can imagine that meticulous professional care is necessary to maintain the best possible condition of his hooves. Without the proper hoof care, it is obvious that the ramifications can be detrimental to your horse.

This professional you will be seeking is commonly called a **farrier**. He or she will visit your horse every few weeks to maintain his hooves and to advise you of any changes that he or she recommends in care.

While farriers are not qualified veterinarians, they work in conjunction with your veterinarian to promote the best possible care for your horse's hoofs. They will also advise you as to what steps you can take to provide the best possible upkeep for your horse's hooves. You should make a point to pay very close attention to instructions that you receive so that you may be as consistent as possible in your methods of care. Remember, abrupt changes can cause problems for your horses. An experienced farrier can be invaluable to you and your horse.

Choosing Your Farrier

Choosing a farrier can sometimes be a difficult process—especially for a new owner. Chances are you may be unaware of what a farrier does and will not understand much of what he may tell you until you've become more seasoned. This makes the process of choosing a farrier that much more difficult, since you will entrust that person with a very big responsibility based upon his or her recommendations and advice.

As will be the case with all the professionals that you employ, you will need to conduct enough research to ensure that you have made the most responsible choice. This process can be a bit time-consuming but will be worth the trouble. Making the wrong choice may later mean correcting a bad situation and correcting any damage to your horse. Therefore, you would be well-advised to make your most informed choice the first time.

I suggest the same techniques in choosing your farrier as you did in choosing your veterinarian. You should be sure to have a personal conversation with any possible prospects, and it is also advisable to check with your state farrier's association (if one exists) to determine whether that person is currently in good standing and whether any formal complaints have been filed with the organization. I also suggest asking for your veterinarian's recommendation in this matter, because he or she will likely know many reputable farriers. Good farriers will work closely with your equine practitioner to ensure your horse's best hoof care. Other experienced owners and your barn manager will also be a great source of suggesting a reputable farrier. Generally, most stable facilities have a particular farrier who visits consistently, and you may find it advantageous to add your horse to his client list.

Once you have conducted the preliminary steps in choosing your farrier, it is time to ask a few more specific questions. What certifications do you hold? How many years of experience do you have? Would you be willing to provide references? Do you know my equine practitioner? These questions are important to you and your horse.

There are three major farrier organizations: *The American Farrier's Association (AFA), The International Association of Professional Farriers (IAPF), and The United States Farrier Association (USFA).* Smaller regional organizations such as *The Brotherhood of Working*

Farriers (BWFA) also certify farriers. These organizations not only certify farriers but also foster collaboration with veterinarians, promote research, and host clinics and conventions. If you're considering certification or looking for a qualified farrier, these are excellent places to start. Some states and regions also have farrier organizations that serve as chapters to and work in tandem with the AFA or IAPF. Should your farrier be certified? My answer is *absolutely*. Are all farriers certified? No. Is being certified a requirement of being a practicing farrier? No. Certification is **not** legally required to work as a farrier in the United States. Farriery is an unregulated profession in most states, meaning anyone can technically offer hoof care services without formal credentials.

Common Roles of State Farrier Associations

- Continuing education clinics and workshops
- Certification prep and testing support
- Networking and mentorship opportunities
- Advocacy for farrier standards and welfare
- Directories of local certified farriers

Examples of State and Regional Associations

- Georgia Professional Farriers Association
- Texas Professional Farriers Association
- California Professional Farriers Association
- Mid-Eastern Farriers Association (covers multiple states)
- New England Farriers Association

In the mid-1990's, I undertook an extensive effort to establish licensing standards for practicing farriers in a proposed legislative bill called: *The Practicing Farrier Certification Act.*

At the time, I interviewed several working farriers—both certified and uncertified—in an effort to gauge their interest and feedback regarding possible licensing requirements. I also spoke to numerous horse owners, state officials, and equine practitioners for their feedback. I discovered that there was not a high level of concern for continuing education in the discipline and even less concern for certification—mainly amongst farriers. Although many farriers attempt to eloquently avoid the issues concerning certification, they are still quick to point out a substantial price list for their services. My main argument in favor of licensing was the fact that farriers deal with live tissue and some of what they do is surgical in nature by any standard.

The resistance to my proposed legislation was exceptionally fierce. As of 2025, no state in the union requires a farrier to be certified; it is totally voluntary on the part of the farrier. The one exception, however, is states that have sanctioned horse racing do require track farriers to be licensed by the applicable state racing commission.

According to 2025 statistics provided by *Zippia*, there are approximately 2,000 to 3,000 certified farriers in the United States, depending on the certifying organization and level of certification. This represents a fraction of the total farrier workforce, which is estimated to be between 20,000 and 25,000 individuals nationwide. Roughly 10%-15% of the total workforce is certified with roughly 75% being male and 25% female.

Therefore, nothing has really changed in three decades with respect to farrier certification. To be transparent, I have used both uncertified and certified farriers in the past—mainly due to geographical constraints or farrier availability. Thankfully, my horse never suffered any real problems that I could attribute to farrier negligence. But I would also note that he also never suffered any serious injuries or conditions that required more than routine trimming and shoeing. He was fortunate in that regard, but I always opted to have a certified farrier if possible. Thankfully, that was the case much of the time.

My position on farriers in 2025 is that you should make every effort to use only a certified farrier if possible. Certified farriers have made a concerted effort to be a professional in their field with utilizing apprenticeships, progressing levels of certification, and ongoing annual continuing education. To put it simply, farriery is a *hard* job. It is very physical and potentially dangerous given what these folks do. In short, I have a lot of respect for the nature of their job and what it takes to attain a high level of expertise—especially in cases where horses experience really challenging issues. Like equine practitioners, farriers do some amazing things to support the health and well-being of horses. And the technical innovation of shoes, materials, adhesives, tools, and techniques enable farriers to do things once unheard of in equine care.

Chapter Five: Stable Facilities

One of the most important aspects of horse ownership and your horse's well-being is their housing and habitat. It plays an extremely important role in your horse's physical and mental health. If he is going to be called upon to perform for you on a regular basis, it only makes sense that the happier he is within his home and environment, the more effective he will be in his duties. Keep in mind that horses are also extremely resilient. While they love pampering, thousands of horses survive in the wild on their own. The truth is that, like dogs and cats and other domesticated animals, horses mainly appreciate good food and attention. Anything else is truly a bonus.

In this chapter, we will concentrate heavily upon stable facilities. We will look closely at points of interest that surround these facilities and their operation as well as the folks that operate them for a living. It is essential that you become familiar with these facilities and their methods of operation so that you may better understand the decision you may undertake with regards to patronizing one of these facilities. I can attest to the fact that looks can sometimes be deceiving when choosing a stable facility, and if you are too hasty and uninformed in making a final decision to patronize that facility, you may regret your decision in the long run.

You may opt to keep your horse on your own property, and that can be the best choice of all, but unfortunately, constraints of one kind or another often prohibit that luxury and convenience. Therefore, we will concentrate on a need for a boarding facility for our purposes of discussion and debate.

<u>Show and Tell</u>

The most effective way to choose a stable facility is to simply travel to as many as possible that meet your needs of proximity and convenience. Keep in mind, however, that the closest facility may not necessarily be the best facility for you. You will be searching for a facility that best meets your specific needs and the needs of your horse.

Without question, you will be required to evaluate certain aspects of a stable facility before you ever make a visit. First, evaluate your own needs regarding activities in which you choose to participate. If you are interested in show jumping, then you will need specific equipment for that activity. Second, decide upon the standard of living that your horse will come to enjoy. You should have certain expectations as to the level of comfort and care that your horse will be given in exchange for your payment. Third, consider what you can realistically afford. It is easy to overextend yourself with a horse, and it is advisable for you to sit down and formulate a working budget that now includes your horse and his upkeep. Also keep in mind that the most expensive facility may not necessarily be the best facility for you. By the same token, you often get exactly what you pay for.

Once you have made these preliminary decisions, it is time for a visit to the stable that interests you. My advice is to call ahead and speak with the barn manager to make an appointment for a facility walk-through. Most facility owners and barn managers are generous when it comes to potential customers and will point you in the right direction. This initial visit will mean many things regarding your final decision. While I used to suggest showing up unannounced, security measures for clients and horses have rightfully increased. So, make an appointment.

It is very important that you understand the concept of stable facilities. These facilities are a place of business. And while I state this fact in the simplest terms, the sooner that you make a differentiation between business and pleasure, the more astute you will become as an owner. As I stated before, there is much to be said about the *profit motive*. Without this motive, there lies little incentive to succeed on the part of the stable facility. Moreover, you are provided with a service that is of importance to you and your horse. Therefore, you pay for your horse's care and housing. By the same token, if a stable facility and its owner are not driven by profit and competition, it is possible that the service you will receive will be short of your expectations.

It is important for you to establish a stable owner's motive for being involved in the equine business. This is essential because unless you have this crucial information, you will be lacking a major detail to consider. In other words, do they operate the facility as a business or simply as supplemental income to subsidize their own horse's care? If it is a combination of both, that is not necessarily a bad thing.

There are many facilities in existence that look somewhat like a home/barn/farm. You may find that the stable facility owners are also homeowners on that particular property. If that is the case, it would be wise to look beyond the fact that someone will be on the property much of the time to watch the horses and decide whether you feel comfortable invading someone's home space. At its essence in this type of arrangement, be advised that you are at the owner's mercy should you have a disagreement or dispute.

I am a firm believer in separating home from business, and if you are faced with a precarious situation due to a disagreement, it can be difficult to approach an owner who also resides on the property. To me, home is not the best place for business and negotiation for the most part. I also feel as if it is far more professional for a businessperson to conduct his or her affairs in a place specifically set aside for that purpose. Notwithstanding, be aware that many operations do business as I described, and should you have a disagreement, moving a horse to another location can be a challenging situation.

This is not to say that farm owners who also operate a stable facility on the farm property are in any way dishonest or deceitful. Chances are that most stable owners that happen to live upon the described property are upstanding and professional. However, there is great merit in suspecting that you may run into one who is problematic. Because you are paying for housing and care for your horse, your expectations are spelled out succinctly. Disputes can and do happen, so try to be as sure as possible that you have a high level of comfort with the circumstances, arrangements, and folks involved when choosing this type of facility.

You should be searching for a facility that has a good reputation based upon your own expectations. As I stated previously, your taste and mine may or may not differ. So, you must establish a standard to follow. It would be advisable for you to search for a facility that has built that reputation over time. I'm a bit more comfortable with a facility that has been in place for some time if possible. By the same token, do not disqualify a new facility or one under new management. You may be pleasantly surprised to find out that the new management is qualified and competent and has admirable plans for the future.

All in all, you should be looking for a facility that appears to operate in a professional manner. The facility should have an office, a business phone listing, and a positive reputation to back it up. Remember that a stable facility is a business, and you are expecting services to be rendered in exchange for payment. I think I've been quite clear in conveying the fact that horse boarding facilities can be quite expensive. So, it is important for you to be thoroughly satisfied with the management, their employees, the appearance of the premises, and the general atmosphere of the facility before you ever commit to boarding your horse there. Generally, horse stables are not only a business, but also somewhat social depending on the atmosphere and clientele. They are a great place to meet new friends with common interests.

Inspection

Once you've narrowed your list of possible boarding facilities, you should be prepared to request a guided tour of the facility and insist upon having an owner or manager with you so that you may introduce any pertinent questions. This process is very important to you because representations will be made on the part of the management or owner regarding services that you may or may not receive as well as conditions set forth that govern you and your horse. I would suggest that you have at least one witness accompanying you so that any pertinent remark may be noted. It might even be preferable to take a friend along (as opposed to a relative) to avoid any accusation of bias should that person need to recount any representations made at a future date. This is for your protection.

You will have to equate the price of monthly board fees to the type of amenities available and the services provided. According to the *Joyful Equestrian*, the typical monthly cost of boarding a horse in the U.S. ranges from $350 *to* $800, but it can vary widely—from as low as $100 to over $2,000—depending on location, services, and amenities.

In all fairness, if you are paying $300 a month for board, you will probably not receive many of the comforts and perks of an $800 facility. Pay what you can afford according to your working budget. It also does not mean that the $300 per month facility is necessarily deficient.

Irrespective of where you choose to stable your horse, there is a minimum that you should expect with respect to the actual stall, the pasture and paddocks, tack and equipment storage, feeding arrangements, etc. These items require inspection, and if you are not satisfied with their appearance and function, you may want to choose another facility. Importantly, these are the basic items that will determine your horse's health and well-being.

Horse Boarding Cost Comparison - *Courtesy of Equine Helper*

Boarding Type	Typical Monthly Cost	Services Included
Self-Care Board	$100–$200	Stall or pasture space only. The owner provides all feed, cleaning, and care.
Pasture Board	$150–$400	Outdoor living with shelter. The facility provides feed and water.
Full-Care Board	$300–$700	Stall, daily feeding, turnout, stall cleaning, and basic care.
Training Board	$800–$2,000+	Full care plus professional training and exercise programs.

Here is a list of items that you need to check firsthand during your inspection. If you are looking at more than one facility, I suggest that you prepare a formal checklist to carry with you during your inspection. This checklist will serve two functions: 1) You will be able to keep your records in order and have the ability to make a visual comparison of the checklist. 2) This will show the owner or manager that you're serious and knowledgeable about what you are doing.

1) **Fencing** - There are many types of fencing available for farm use. You will likely see wooden rail fence, wooden slat fence, split rail fence, vinyl safety fence, wire fence, barbed wire fence, or variations thereof. Fencing is very important because many injuries occur because of poor-quality or improperly installed or maintained fencing. Horses often roll while in the paddock or pasture, and for some reason, they often roll very near the fence. Much of the time, this makes little sense considering that there are open available spaces, but this is often the case. The horse can become caught (or cast) in the fence and suffer injuries that can even cause the horse to have to be destroyed.

Wooden rail fences are adequate for lining pasture or paddock. They're usually round without sharp edges and can be slid out of the post for a replacement or to free a trapped horse. Often, the rails are lined with electric wire fans to ensure that the horses stay clear of the fence. One problem with wooden fences, though, is that a horse can be injured if he spooks and tries to run through the fence. Obviously, the fence can splinter or may not break at all, possibly causing injury in both cases.

All in all, wood fencing is acceptable if it is maintained and mounted securely. It is classic and attractive if maintained.

Vinyl safety fencing is the best fencing, in my opinion. This fencing has been designed so that it will not splinter or develop sharp edges. It is also designed so that in the event that a horse collides with it, the horse will likely be repelled by the recoil of the wire inserts within the structural body of the slats. Vinyl fencing is also very presentable and low maintenance, but it is also very costly.

If this type of fencing is used at a facility that meets all your criteria, you are very fortunate as this is a definite plus for you and your horse.

Wire fencing is used by many stable facilities as their main source of fencing. This is not something that I recommend. This type of fencing is not very visible and often breaks. It is very easy for a horse to collide with this type of fencing and to become entangled within it—sometimes causing horrific injuries. This fencing should be kept at a designated tension and should also have highly visible color markers in place if it is used as primary fencing.

Wire fencing is also sometimes used as a secondary fencing mechanism in conjunction with other fence types and is usually placed behind rail or vinyl fencing and is electrified to effectively contain the horses. When this type of fencing is used in this way, it is usually attached within an inch or two of the primary fence line. I do not object to this use if it is properly installed, maintained, and highly visible.

Barbed wire fencing is sometimes used and is just too harsh for horses, in my opinion. It is too easy for a horse to injure itself on barbed wire, and if he becomes entangled, you may not like the results. I do not recommend this type of fencing if it is avoidable.

Another variation of wire fencing is chain link fencing. This type of fencing is acceptable but not necessarily recommended. It is not very attractive and does offer the remote possibility of a horse becoming entangled in the link. Some risk does exist, but if no option is available, this fencing will suffice.

In short, fencing is very important to your horse because he or she will spend a great deal of time during their life with a fence serving as a boundary of safety and security. Do your best to make sure that her fencing is at least adequate, and if any defects exist, point them out at once to the barn manager.

2)   **Feeding and Watering Devices** - Throughout the barn stalls and pasture, you will find feeding and watering apparatuses. Obviously, your horse will ingest food and water from these devices throughout the day.

Your horse's feeder may take many shapes and sizes, but essentially the feeder holds food for the horse, and the animal eats directly from the feeder. A feeder should be, above all else, clean and sanitary. If not, your horse is susceptible to bacteria and parasites that may be harmful to his health. Feeders can be as simple as a shallow bucket or a more permanently mounted corner or trough feeder. Generally, horses are not picky as long as they get tasty nutritious food. Above all else, a feeder should be clean and sanitary to prevent ingestion of bacteria and parasites. Naturally, they should be washed and sanitized regularly and replaced when they become too porous.

As hay is important to a horse's diet, you should also see a mounted hay rack in barn stalls. Some owners opt for a hay net instead. In either case, both allow the horse to ingest hay that is kept off the ground and uncontaminated. If nets are used, it is preferable that they be hung in a corner to minimize any chance of the horse becoming entangled and injured. Both are acceptable, but a mounted hay rack is preferred.

Make sure to look at watering devices around the property. They will be located within the individual barn stalls and within paddock areas. Most facilities have opted for automatic waterers that are operated by a float or pressure mechanism that provides fresh water as the horses drink. Not only is the water fresher, but the devices are eco-friendly and save water. Heating elements are also often utilized during the winter months to keep the water from freezing.

Standing water tubs are often used in pastures as a water source. It is advisable that these tubs are aerated to prevent algae growth and insect infestation. Automatic filling systems can also be utilized in standing tubs bringing fresh water into the supply as the horses drink.

While horses tend to be resilient, clean water and sanitary food delivery systems go a long way to promote your horse's good health. So, pay close attention to these items during your initial inspection of the facility.

3)   **Paddock and Pasture Areas** - Your horse will likely spend at least 50% of his time out to pasture—possibly even more. Whereby, the condition of his pasture area is crucial to good health and well-being. In this area, he will graze, exercise, socialize with other horses, ride out storms, and play. These activities constitute much of the time that he spends in your absence.

Grazing is very important to horses. The grass contains vitamins, minerals, and roughage that are essential to their digestive system. If your horse is kept in a pasture, at least one acre should be reserved for him—even one-and-a-half if possible. To put it in simpler terms, at least one acre of pasture per horse within the pasture is ideal. This provides ample space to avoid conflicts between horses and allows for the pasture not to be overused by those horses populating the area.

Pastures should be clean, and the grass should be lush. Also take into consideration what part of the country in which you reside and the types of grasses common to that region. If conditions of a drought exist, you should insist that the pasture be watered if possible. Also inquire as to what chemicals and fertilizers are used and if they are potentially harmful to horses.

During your inspection of the paddocks and pasture, see to it that they are not overcrowded and overused. I recall one farm that had no grass whatsoever in the paddocks and sometimes kept as many as 22 horses within a one-acre area. This is unacceptable. If adequate space is unavailable, that facility is remiss to continue overcrowding the area with more horses. But some stable facilities will pack as many horses into the area as possible with no regard for health hazards or the grazing that horses need. Unfortunately, this can be a result of poor farm management and an overzealous desire to put profit ahead of the well-being of the horses.

Make certain that pastures are free of dangerous obstacles that may potentially injure an animal. It may take some extra time to inspect the entire pasture, but I advise going to the trouble and giving it a frequent walk-through. There are often nails, glass, stumps, protruding sticks, and rocks that may prove hazardous to you and your horse. As I mentioned previously, make sure that all fences are up to par as well.

Lastly, your local Department of Agriculture is usually happy to test the soil and grass within the pastures from your prospective farm. They can tell you what minerals are lacking or if the grass is optimal for grazing. They may also be able to tell you what fertilizers and pesticides are used and provide directions that you should follow regarding their use. This is a very useful service, and you should take advantage of the technology available.

4)   **Feed Rooms and Storage Areas** - These areas are commonly used to store your horse's food and supplements. Obviously, you should be sure that these areas are free of insects, rodents, and other animals that may contaminate foodstuffs and supplements. It is easy to understand that rodent droppings can cause illness to your horse and serious sickness that might otherwise be avoided with good storage habits.

If traps or chemicals are used to deter rodent infestation, make certain that any chemical or bait is kept away from the horses guarding against food contamination and accidental poisoning.

There are two major 24/7 animal poisoning hotlines in the U.S.: the ASPCA Animal Poison Control Center (888-426-4435) and the Pet Poison Helpline (855-764-7661). Both provide expert toxicology advice for pets who may have ingested harmful substances. A consultation fee may apply for these services and is around $100.

Inspect any storage containers that house the actual feed. These containers may take many shapes, but whatever type of storage container is used, it should be clean and sealed to keep flies and rodents out. If you're dissatisfied with the current containers, you may opt to provide your own. Many horse owners often provide their own storage containers and feed instructions. Don't hesitate to do so if you feel more confident. This avoids mistakes and miscommunication.

In short, the feed room is your horse's kitchen. If it is not kept clean and sanitary, you may eventually see that it can be harmful to the horses. All spills should be cleaned immediately, and all foodstuffs should be securely contained to avoid contamination. It has been my general experience that stable facilities are pretty consistent about making sure that food is free of contaminants, but the reality is that rodents love barns. That's why you often see the ubiquitous barn cats or Jack Russell Terriers who revel in helping keep barns free of rodents.

5)   **Bedding** - Your horse's barn stall will serve as his shelter and safe space when he is not out to pasture. He will spend a great deal of time there, so the bedding that is used within his stall is very important to his well-being and comfort.

There are many methods of stall construction, and there are as many opinions as to what construction is best. Since horses usually stand while in their stall, it only makes sense that the floor is constructed in such a fashion as providing stability and comfort. Floors are generally constructed of concrete, brick, sand, clay, dirt, or a combination thereof. In my opinion, stable but pliable materials are best because they are flexible to weight. When concrete or brick is used, mats constructed of rubber or recycled tires are often used for padding. Your horse needs a stable but comfortable foundation.

Over the floor, bedding material is used. Bedding material ranges from sawdust to wood shavings to straw to shredded paper. Bedding provides a place for him to lay down and an area in which waste is deposited. For that reason, the material should be versatile enough to accommodate moisture.

1) Sawdust is acceptable. It is soft, absorbent and smells nice, but it can create a dusty climate that does not stand up well to prolonged moisture. 2) Straw is acceptable, but the horse may try to eat it and risks ingesting a contaminated area. Straw does not stand up well to moisture such as urine. 3) Wood shavings are my personal choice of bedding material. Shavings tend to eliminate dusty conditions, hold urine contained in one spot and smell good—especially cedar shavings. Shavings are also easy to maintain with regards to waste removal and can be completely replaced or supplemented with new shavings at any time. Wood shavings are also soft and give the horse a secure bed in case he decides to lay down. 4) Lastly, shredded paper is a choice but not highly recommended for horses. While it

does have advantageous use in livestock management, it isn't ideal for your horse. This material tends to become impacted in a horse's hooves, lacks structure for support, becomes very compact with any moisture, and is not receptive to urine and droppings. While this material is cheap and recycled, it is the worst material to use for bedding and should only be used in a pinch and not for a long period of time.

During your inspection, take a close look at the bedding used and the condition of the existing material. Again, *sanitary* is the operative term. Bedding should be changed or supplemented as often as needed. Also, make sure that floors within the stalls are leveled, and lime can be used to neutralize frequently used urine spots. A clean, sanitary stall is one that should satisfy you and will certainly satisfy your horse.

6)   **Riding Areas** - You and your horse will spend a lot of time within the areas designated for riding and training. These areas may take many shapes and forms such as rings, covered arenas, indoor arenas, ovals, trails, and courses. Riding areas are a very important component in your stable choice, and you should be sure that all areas necessary to your needs meet certain criteria.

First and foremost, riding areas should be designed to promote safety. In your initial inspection, determine whether any dangerous obstacles or hazards exist within that area. Remember that riding is inherently risky at the outset, but there should not exist any unnecessary additional hazards that increase that risk.

The riding surface, itself, is also of importance to you and your horse. Determine what the surface consists of and how it reacts to certain conditions. There are several surfaces used by facilities usually dependent upon budget. Examples of surfaces are clay, dirt, sand, dirt and sand mixture, sawdust, wood shavings, grass, or synthetic material like ground rubber.

Horses have historically traversed all types of surfaces—from very rough to very comfortable—but remember that hooves can become damaged from a surface that is not suitable, and other injuries can occur from surfaces that are dangerous. I really have no problem with any surface for pleasure and competitive riding, although deep sand can be problematic.

For the most part, riding areas should be designed to drain properly and to maintain their form and composure. Inquire as to whether there are any drainage problems and how soon after a rain you may be able to comfortably and safely use the area. If dusty conditions persist, ask whether a sprinkler system is in place to suppress the dust. Also check to see if night riding is allowed and if adequate lighting is in place. During the winter months when the days are shorter, you may come to depend on artificial lighting so that you can ride. If you are fortunate enough to have a facility that operates an indoor arena, make sure that approved lighting is in place for your safety.

Please consider these points relating to riding areas before you make your final decision. You and your horse will be greatly dependent on these areas and will spend a great deal of time practicing and honing your skills within them.

7)   **Staff Employees** - Probably the most important factor in determining whether you want to patronize a stable facility are their employees who will be responsible for your horse. When you think of other folks caring for the needs of your horse, it is natural to feel some concern and apprehension. Consider that when you are not at the stable facility, someone else will be responsible for feeding her, administering light first aid, exercising her, safely transferring her from one area to another, providing any medication or supplements important to her health, and any other prescribed duties of relevance. There is a great deal of responsibility taken on by stable facilities, their management, and employees. Horse care is not an exact science, so we want to get it right.

Spend an ample amount of time simply watching facility employees handle their responsibilities. Watch how they handle the horses. Observe the level of care that they take in feeding, bathing, and exercising the horses. Examine their rapport with other employees. Is there a sense of cooperation between them? Is there an evident sense of pride in their work? Do they follow the directions of the owners, veterinarians, and management? Do they appear to like the work they do? These are all questions that should be addressed. Proceed with your best intuition. With regards to staff on hand at a facility, do not be afraid to ask management if background checks have been conducted on employees and do some online research with respect to character and reputation. Due diligence will help ensure your horse's safety and your own.

8)   **Safety and Security** - As I stated, safety is the foremost concern for you and your horse. If a facility has little concern for the safety issues concerning horse owners, spectators, and the horses, you should avoid that facility regardless of the amenities. Again, there is a happy medium between profit and ethical obligation.

Some facilities may insist that you follow proscribed rules of conduct with regards to safety-related issues. For example, a facility may require you to always wear protective headgear when mounted on your horse. They may require that you wear approved safety footwear when riding. They may require that your horse be cross-tied when in the barn area and out of his stall unless you have him in-hand. You may be prohibited from riding after sunset if lighting is not in place. These rules would not be unreasonable and show a level of responsibility on the part of the facility. Ask for a list of safety rules issued to new boarders and review them thoroughly. You may even be required to attend a safety class for new patrons.

Another legitimate concern for you and your horse is security measures instituted at the facility. Some facilities may have twenty-four hours of armed security, a coded security gate, motion sensor lighting, and day/night camera surveillance. Of course, the level of security that your horse receives will probably fall in line with your monthly boarding fee—although the cost of electronic surveillance has become *far* more affordable. Notwithstanding, you express your concern over facility security and have management explain their security features.

Lastly, find a stable facility that has a fire prevention/suppression system in place if at all possible. This is especially important if the owners or managers are not on the property full-time—although some facilities do have an employee living onsite.

If you have ever seen a movie that depicted a barn fire and the chaotic reaction of horses, you can readily relate to my point. Ideally, I suggest a facility that has a sprinkler system in place. In my opinion, the cost of these systems is modest compared to the potential property damage and anguish that would result if a fire could have been prevented or suppressed. Personally, I believe that all commercial stable facilities should be required to have a sprinkler system in place, but not all do. Make yourself familiar with fire extinguisher locations at the facility just in case.

Safety and security should be at the top of your list when considering a facility. If proper measures are not in place, ask some questions and make a friendly suggestion. The proprietor may shrug them off, but rest assured that your concerns have merit. Remember, your horse is a part of your family, and while a facility owner has profit on his or her mind, you must protect your interests. A responsible owner or manager will welcome your concerns.

9)   **Health Record** - Another important factor to consider when choosing a stable is to examine the health and medical record of that facility. If, for example, the facility has had prior problems with parasitical infections, you should investigate as to the cause of the problem and if the facility was responsible. You should also inquire as to how many accidents occurred on the property and how many resulted in injuries to the riders and to the horses. Attempt to locate any record of infectious disease that may have resulted in quarantines or the deaths of horses. Find out how many accidents have occurred with horses in transit to and from the facility and if fault was that of the employer or owner if possible.

If you think that this information is difficult to obtain or intrusive, you may be right. However, I would investigate anyway. It may take some extra time, but it is of importance to you and your horse. Thankfully, the internet makes this research more accessible to acquire. I would also encourage you to contact the State Veterinarian Office to see if any prior problems have been documented by that office or if any formal complaints have been lodged against the facility.

The better the safety and health record, the better off you and your horse will be in the long run. Approach these issues in a friendly, non-confrontational way with any facility owner or manager to simply express concern. Do your best to stack the odds in your favor from the beginning by ensuring that good health records are predominant at that facility. In all fairness, stable owners cannot prevent all things, but you should feel confident that they are doing their best to mitigate any potential problems.

10)   **Maintenance Schedules** - As a new horse owner, you will come to find that one of the major elements in care for your horse is *consistency*. Without consistency, you can put your horse at risk of health problems. This is the primary reason that an established schedule of maintenance should be implemented by your stable facility and should be followed as set forth by you and your equine practitioner.

Maintenance refers to feeding, worming, supplements, medications, and anything that is given at specified periods of time. These intervals may be daily, weekly, or otherwise, but should be followed accordingly. You should consult your equine practitioner for dietary advice concerning your horse. After you have established preliminary information such as the chemical balance of the available grass and ground cover, you will need to know what sources and amounts of nutrition your horse will need. It has been said that feeding is as much of an art as it is a science. This is not totally off base. Your equine practitioner may instruct you to implement a certain feeding schedule that will be reevaluated in a month or so and adjusted accordingly.

Worming and parasite control are also an essential part of your horse's maintenance schedule. Most wormers are delivered in either a paste, granule, or pellet form. Parasite control will ensure that your horse will not be infested and that he or she will maintain good health and physical condition. Naturally, if your horse is treated regularly, you'll want to make sure that all other horses are also on a deworming regimen. Most owners realize this is a healthy routine.

You may also rest assured that if you are going to board at a professionally operated facility that you will be required to provide a record of a **Coggins Test** and other inoculation records for any infectious disease that is treated under mandate by the state in which you reside. A Coggins Test is a blood test used to detect **Equine Infectious Anemia (EIA).** It is a contagious and potentially fatal viral disease in horses, mules, ponies, and donkeys. It's required for interstate travel, competitions, sales, and boarding to prevent outbreaks. You'll need this test for traveling across state lines, attending competitions or events, boarding at equine facilities, and selling or purchasing horses. Consider it as a passport for your horse.

According to the (AAEP), horses are required to receive these core vaccines every year: *Tetanus, Rabies, Eastern/Western Equine Encephalomyelitis (EEE/WEE)*, and *West Nile Virus*. Additional risk-based vaccines (like *Equine Influenza, Equine Herpesvirus, and Strangles*) may be recommended depending on travel, boarding, or regional risks.

Core Vaccines (Required for All Horses)

These are considered essential by the **American Association of Equine Practitioners (AAEP)** because they protect against widespread, life-threatening diseases:

- Tetanus – Caused by soil bacteria; nearly always fatal without vaccination.
- Rabies – Fatal zoonotic disease; required by law in many states.
- Eastern & Western Equine Encephalomyelitis (EEE/WEE) – Mosquito-borne viruses causing severe neurological disease.
- West Nile Virus – Another mosquito-borne virus leading to neurological illness and death.

Risk-Based Vaccines (Given Depending on Exposure)

These are recommended based on your horse's lifestyle, travel, and environment:

- Equine Influenza – Highly contagious respiratory disease; common in show and travel horses.
- Equine Herpesvirus (EHV-1 & EHV-4) – Causes respiratory illness, abortion in mares, and neurological disease.
- Strangles – Bacterial infection of lymph nodes; spreads rapidly in barns.
- Botulism – Risk in areas with contaminated feed or soil.
- Potomac Horse Fever – Regional disease linked to aquatic insects; common in certain U.S. states.
- Rotavirus – Protects foals against severe diarrhea.

Typical Vaccination Schedule

- **Core vaccines:** Annually, often in spring before mosquito season.
- **Risk-based vaccines:** Every 6–12 months depending on exposure (e.g., influenza every 6 months for traveling horses).
- **Foals:** Begin vaccinations at 4–6 months, with boosters 4 weeks later.

Why Vaccination Matters

- **Prevents fatal diseases** with no cure (EEE, Rabies, Tetanus).
- **Protects herd health** in boarding barns and competitions.
- **Required for travel, shows, and sales** (proof of vaccination often needed).

Maintenance schedules are of the utmost importance to you and your horse. You will be amazed at the information that a documented schedule and daily journal can provide. Veterinary experts and farriers can use this valuable information to assist in the diagnosis of problems that may be related to maintenance changes or lack of maintenance. This may seem like a complicated and time-consuming effort, but keep in mind that horses cannot talk. So, the more accurate information that you have available to analyze, the more valuable it may be in the future to your veterinarian. Most stables utilize a simple dry erase board to list exactly what your horse gets and when. Pretty simple and effective.

11)   **The Stall** - When your horse is not out to pasture, his stall is where your horse will call home. Horses tend to prefer a lush pasture, shade trees, cool water, and his pasture mates to the indoors, but also enjoy the sense of security that a well-constructed stall offers. However, stalls are important to owners to be able to more effectively monitor nutritional intake, bumps and scratches, and water intake. And most horses enjoy the security of a comfortable stall and shelter.

Safety is the number one concern of any horse owner when considering a stall. You should be extra vigilant when it comes to inspecting a stall for protruding nails, large splinters, hooks, twine, loose wire and any other obstacles that can cause an injury. One problem within the stall environment is that your horse can panic. When he feels trapped, he can become extremely claustrophobic and take flight away from his perceived danger. In this situation, there is no place for a horse to escape. During this panic process, the horse can obviously become injured, so the less chance there is for him to injure himself on an obstacle within the stall, the better it will be for him. These situations are atypical but can happen.

Stall sanitation is one point that cannot be stressed enough. You will find that horses are so patient when it comes to poor conditions, but that doesn't mean they should be exposed to that. Manure removal is essential and should be initiated one to two times per day. Manure should be disposed of in a distant location and should be covered if possible. Most stable facilities have an area designated for just that purpose. Keep in mind that the stall floor is just part of the equation. All too often, people forget the walls, ceilings, fixtures, et cetera. The cleaner the stall, the less chance of flies, parasites, fungus, bacteria, and rodents. Horses will lie down in the most unsanitary of conditions, so make sure that you and the facility staff are keeping his stall tidy.

Respiratory disease is one of the leading killers of horses. As I stated previously, their systems are sensitive to many things that are foreign to them. Therefore, when considering whether a stall is appropriately constructed, you should take ventilation into account. As strong and resilient as horses are, their systems are somewhat fragile, and their breathing mechanisms are susceptible to infection. With these facts in mind, proper ventilation is a must in helping to maintain your horse's health.

The stall walls should be constructed of quality hardwood if possible. Oak is a very good hardwood for this situation. It is chew-resistant, very attractive, and will stand up to punishment. Wood also breathes better than most other construction materials. If wood is not used, construction may consist of concrete block walls, masonry brick, metal, or some combination thereof. All in all, a stall should always be clean, comfortable, safe, well-ventilated and conscientiously maintained.

Stalls come in many sizes. and regardless of where you happen to board your horse, there will likely be advantages and disadvantages to the stalls available. The perfect stall is somewhat relative, so be your own judge. Your horse should have enough room to turn around, lay down, and expend waste without discomfort. Experiment with his environment. If he gets a chill often, maybe there is a draft. In this case, you may consider a blanket. If his nose runs and he gags often, there may be a ventilation issue. A fan may help. If he experiences hock sores, check the thickness of his bedding. If he is chewing the walls or stall door, it may help to get a play ball to keep him occupied. Over time, you'll become more familiar with your horse's quirks and personality and be better equipped to address his needs with the help of your stable employees.

Lastly, be prepared that you may have that special horse who prefers to be outside most of the time. Some horses will be rotated in for feeding and make it well-known that they are ready to go right back outside when they finish. Don't worry, they just prefer being outside.

In the Business

When it is all said and done, you will be dealing with people instead of hypotheticals and theories. Much of your satisfaction or displeasure will come from the success of communication between you and your prospective boarding facility. To ensure your success and satisfaction, seek out a facility that meets your reasonable and informed expectations.

In the horse business, your expectations should be high but realistic given the fact that maintaining a horse can be quite expensive. Naturally, your individual arrangement is subjective to the needs of you and your horse, so nothing is carved of stone. Simply examine what services will be rendered by the facility, what duties you may or may not undertake, and the cost of what is provided. If all details are spelled out and you feel comfortable with the arrangement, proceed with confidence and enjoy the experience. All efforts to avoid any misunderstanding or miscommunication will make the experience much more pleasurable—just like any other business arrangement.

The equine industry is a commercial enterprise like all other commercial enterprises, and we can all agree that they will perform a service and be compensated accordingly. Some stable facilities will be larger and provide more amenities and services while other facilities may be family-owned and offer their own choice of services on a more nominal scale. This is not to say that any one facility is *better* than the other—*better* must be defined by you, the consumer. But understand that businesses have operating expenses, overhead costs, legal and professional fees, etc. Therefore, you must be able to equate price to what services and amenities are worth to you.

As with all businesses, there are substandard facility owners and operators. They may only be concerned with personal gain, a fast buck, or taking advantage of the uninformed consumer. It has been my experience that these types of people can and do exist and should be avoided. What is more unfortunate, though, is that as a new or potentially new horse owner, you may not be equipped with the knowledge to determine a good situation from a bad one. Believe me, this author has been in that position. Being prepared is the key to success.

In Chapter One, we discussed the term *"professional"* and those who make that claim versus who qualifies. Many of the folks with whom you will come into contact when searching for a facility may claim to be just that. Unfortunately, the terms *"professional"* and *"expert"* are used loosely in the equine business.

I recall dealing with one stable owner who proudly stated that *"he had thirty years in the business and was an expert..."* While I have above-average proficiency in dealing with legal issues, that doesn't make me an attorney. While a paramedic has proficiency with emergency medical triage, that does not make him/her a physician. The point being that while our *"thirty years in the business"* expert clearly had a solid foundation in the horse business, making the *"expert"* claim was, at the very least, risky and misleading.

There is no concrete prerequisite required for being in business for yourself. Within a free market economy, all of us have a unique opportunity to operate our own enterprise unless special qualifications are required by law. However, you should clarify exactly what experience and educational qualifications a so-called *expert* or *professional* possess before you entrust your affairs and your horse to that person. Professional certifications are not required in the horse business unless they are related to sanctioned racing. It is not my intention to overstate the issue; I simply want to again encourage you to do your due diligence and to exercise caution.

My advice is not to be afraid to verify what you have been told. If a person makes claims of having a high level of expertise, simply ask some probing questions and let them explain. Ask them if they hold any special certifications. You may even want to ask for a reference. As with anything else, always be cautious when taking someone's word in a situation like this. You do not want you or your horse to suffer the consequences later. Keep in mind that there *are* honest, hardworking people in the business who are genuinely concerned with you and the welfare of your horse. Whether it is a small family-owned farm with six stalls or an opulent riding club, the goals are to be safe, have fun, and give your horse a great life.

Commercial Responsibility

In Chapter Three, we discussed the necessity of proper insurance at length. Hopefully after reading that chapter, you had a clear understanding of the fact that insurance should be in place for your protection and for the protection of others. With that premise in mind, consider the importance of a stable owner having the proper coverage in place. Any potential stable facility that you consider should readily provide proof of commercial liability insurance upon request. If they refuse to divulge that information, I might suggest that you steer clear of that facility. Please be advised that this question may be contentious to a smaller facility owner, as some of them may rely solely on their state equine liability immunity laws in lieu of the proper insurance.

Every commercial enterprise is at risk in one way or another and would be remiss not to carry proper insurance coverage. To be fair, it is likely that the facility has done the right thing and does maintain a commercial liability policy, but smaller family-owned facilities may not. In the equine industry where inherent risk is present by default, patronizing a facility that does not have the proper insurance coverage in place to protect you and other horses, patrons, visitors, property is simply asking for legal problems. If you become injured because of the facility's negligence, you have a right to be compensated for your injuries, hospitalization, and other related expenses. That is simply part of the cost of doing business, but some facilities may solely depend on the implied immunity of state equine liability laws.

If a facility owner does not have the proper coverage in place, we would refer to him or her as commercially irresponsible. It is obvious that he or she is not concerned with the welfare of others and only in making profit. A responsible business owner, however, realizes that accidents can and do happen. Hopefully, he or she opts to have the proper insurance in place. This is not only for your protection, but also for the protection of the facility. The reality is that if a facility is negligent in some way that requires legal action on your behalf, it isn't a personal attack, but rather an action against their insurer. Some owners may not see it that way, but that is nonetheless reality. While you may admire the owner or facility management, you do have to protect your own interests. Again, this is part of the cost of doing business.

On the Dotted Line

Before you choose to enter into any stable agreement, you should be ready to sign a contract of some kind. Do not be alarmed if you are handed a document to be signed. In fact, you should feel a bit more comfortable with the fact that the facility and its management are responsible professionals. Finally, they understand that an agreement should be reduced to writing. In other words, you are entering into a formal agreement. Realize, however, that this contract may not meet your expectations regarding conditions set forth within the document. Moreover, the contract may be constructed in a fashion to give all the advantages to the facility and its owners.

Since you will be expected to sign a formal agreement of some kind prior to patronizing that facility, you should be prepared to carefully review the document and interpret the clauses and conditions therein. Once you have what you feel is a clear understanding of the document, then I would advise you to have your family attorney give it a quick review and interpretation just to be safe. Generally, contracts are a good thing and are used for a specific reason. Keep in mind that chances are more than likely that an attorney prepared the facility contract, and I guarantee you that a preventative approach is an intelligent approach in this regard.

If the terms of a contract do not suit you or your legal counsel, remember that contracts are usually negotiable. There's no reason that an agreement cannot be customized to become more suitable to you while also being acceptable to management. By the same token, you must be prepared to either sign the contract presented to you or choose another facility if the owner will not negotiate the terms. In either case, be prepared from the outset. Do not under any circumstance compromise yourself or your horse if you or your attorney feels that any point within the contract is not within your best interest. Remember that a *fair* agreement must make sense to both parties.

Lastly, keep in mind that many smaller facilities may not conduct business so formally. They may not require any written agreement and simply operate on advising you of the general terms and a handshake. This is not necessarily a reason to avoid the facility outright if expectations, terms, and communication are clear and positive. Unfortunately, you just can't load your horse up in your car and seek out another facility. Use your best judgement and trust your gut.

In Conclusion

Stable facilities are a very useful tool in the life of your horse. You will have an opportunity to make new friends and to increase your level of knowledge by learning from those around you. This will also be a great opportunity for your horse. A good facility that provides comfortable shelter, nutritious food, exercise areas, a safe environment, security, and a broad range of services will keep your horse healthy and in good spirits. In turn, you will reap the rewards that horsemanship has to offer.

Most people that are in business for a living realize that without you, the consumer, they could potentially lose their livelihood. For that reason, most business owners do everything possible to retain you as a customer and make sure that you are satisfied with their job performance. On the other hand, rest assured that there are stable facilities that could seemingly care less whether you are content or not. This has always disturbed me.

Being involved in business myself, I have seen a steady decline in customer satisfaction over the past few years. I've been involved with many businesses that have lost many customers and revenue because their customer service was so poor. Worse, the attitude of management was only selfishly indicative of their own salary, not the satisfaction of their customers. Businesses die in this way, and we are all victims.

I would advise you to seek out a facility where management has proven itself to be customer-oriented in the past and look to stay that way in the future. There is no use for you to spend your hard-earned money at an establishment that does not truly appreciate your business and who takes time to ask for your feedback and address your concerns. This does not mean that a bigger facility is better than a smaller one regarding the personal attention you receive, but it does mean that you should be comfortable with the service you receive overall. It may very well be the case that you simply want the proscribed duties performed as agreed upon with little or no personal contact—which is your prerogative. But many owners love businesses that go the extra mile for them and their horses.

While I am hopeful that your chosen facility is a fantastic choice, I would suggest that you always have a backup facility in place just in case your present relationship becomes strained or terminated for any reason. Facility choices are typically limited by sheer numbers or geography depending upon where you reside. When you only have two or three acceptable facilities available in an area, you are somewhat limited. It is not as easy as one might think to simply move your horse on a whim, so always be prepared just in case.

The prerequisite to any successful business relationship is to be well-researched, conservative when necessary, aggressive when called upon, and intelligent in the choices that you make. Do not give yourself or your horse any reason to suffer from a bad choice or preventable circumstances. If you do make a regrettable decision, take heed, learn from your mistake, and move forward with your new project. A bad day can be remedied by spending time with your horse.

Chapter Six: Instruction and Training

If you are new to the equine business as an owner or potential owner, one consideration that will weigh heavily in your pre-purchase and ownership decision is instruction and training. Instruction and training will soon prove to be an integral part of your experience as an owner, rider, or competitor. Without proper training and instruction, you may find that you do not possess the necessary skills and experience to accomplish your goals. In this case, it is important to employ a professional that possesses the many required qualities, expertise, and experience to advise you or to point you in the right direction.

In this chapter, we will explore the requirements, qualifications, rapport, expertise, education, and experience that makes a trainer appropriate for the task. We will scrutinize what qualities that you will be seeking, the type of relationship that you will have with a trainer, and how you will define success. This can be a difficult process of elimination for you to undertake, but this process is one of extreme importance to you and your horse.

Much of what your horse will learn with regards to habits, movements, disposition, vices, personality, and spirit can and will be directly influenced by your trainer/instructor. If you purchase a horse at a later age in life, many of these qualities will already be shaped and instilled in the horse, but a trainer will nonetheless play a big role in his future behavior and habits. For those reasons, you should exercise good judgment in making that choice. If you are purchasing a "green" horse, there is a little question that those formative first experiences will shape him for the rest of his life. As you probably suspect, choosing the wrong person for the job can be devastating to your efforts and to your wallet.

You may be asking *"what makes a trainer a trainer?"* That is a great question and one that should be addressed. Unfortunately, if you want to advertise yourself as a "horse trainer," there is nothing that prevents you from doing so. As is the case with so many other horse-related titles, there is no real concrete qualification that is required for you to be called a "trainer." This is a definite glitch in the industry and one that I would like to see addressed. Horse riding instructors and trainers are *not legally required* to be certified in most places, but certification is strongly encouraged and often expected by professional organizations, riding schools, and camps.

Currently, there is little excuse for someone to make false claims regarding their qualifications as a trainer or instructor. Yet there are people at your local stables who may do just that. What prevents them from making such a claim? Unfortunately, nothing. Therefore, it is incumbent upon you to employ a high standard for your sake and for the sake of your horse. Thoroughly verify all claims made on behalf of a trainer or instructor to see that that person is honest and forthright and is not misrepresenting themselves to simply obtain your business. I can tell you from experience that you will likely discover false claims made by trainers. This is unfortunate but is often reality. Be prepared and be alert. Your welfare and that of your horse is dependent upon your decision.

Instructor Certification

The horse world is blessed with excellent riders and teachers who are more than willing to teach their philosophy to any student who will pay for the service? Of course, expert instruction is invaluable to an owner and should be relied upon to transform you and your horse into a tight, smooth-running mechanism. The problem is, who possesses the qualifications to teach and train you? Does a wall full of ribbons and trophies qualify an instructor or trainer? It is unfortunate, but just about anyone can claim to be qualified, and the new owner probably does not possess the knowledge to know the difference. It is not enough that a trainer is teaching a system. They must understand the theory and be able to effectively employ the fundamentals of teaching to be effective. The wall of ribbons and the *"thirty years of experience"* are simply not sufficient for our purposes.

Every time you go to a public pool, lifeguards are supervising your activities to ensure safety and compliance with pool rules. Water safety instructors who teach all levels of swimming and lifesaving are employed to teach the proper fundamentals and safety rules. Every time you attend a sporting contest, you observe referees and officials who enforce the rules of the game. Every time you walk into a school classroom, you see a teacher at the head of the class. All these people have one thing in common---they are all properly certified and credentialed. In my opinion, trainers and instructors should be certified as well.

Horsemanship is not a discipline that is simplistic. It is a very complicated area in which few are educated and hold proper credentials. According to *Horsey Hooves,* there are dozens of higher learning institutions that offer equine management and riding education programs. Lists compiled by equestrian education resources typically highlight 15–20 top colleges and universities, but when you include smaller schools, community colleges, and universities with equestrian teams or equine science majors, the number expands to well over 100 institutions nationwide.

In other words, there are available avenues for one to get a formal education. Since that is the case, I would expect those who command handsome prices for their services to have a formal education in the discipline. In addition, we will discuss the numerous certification bodies available that educate trainers, instructors, and facility managers. Notwithstanding the availability, many self-described trainers and instructors hold no formal equine education or certifications.

Ideally, every trainer and instructor with whom you came into contact has a formal equine education and proper credentials that truly qualify that person to train you and your horse. Although there is no legal mandate that trainers or instructors hold any formal certifications, I suggest seeking one out who does. As I have noted many times already, equine activity is inherently dangerous and is complex by nature. I feel resolved that anyone teaching riders and horses should have the credentials to back it up.

Certification demonstrates competence, safety awareness, and professionalism, but whether it is mandatory depends on the country, state, or specific program. Groups like the ***American Riding Instructors Association (ARIA), Certified Horsemanship Association (CHA),*** and ***United States Hunter Jumper Association (USHJA)*** provide structured certification programs. For therapeutic or adaptive riding, organizations such as ***PATH Intl.*** require instructors to be certified to ensure safety and proper training for riders with disabilities

According to the *American Riding Instructors Association*, the following are a few examples of educational programs available to individuals seeking to earn certification in several disciplines.

Examples of Certification Programs

Organization	Focus	Certification Highlights
ARIA	General riding instruction	16 specialties (dressage, distance riding, etc.); emphasizes safety and horsemanship
CHA	English/Western riding, trail guides, facility managers	Evaluates instructors in safety, teaching ability, and horsemanship
USHJA	Hunter/Jumper trainers	Trainer Certification Program (sunsetting in 2025); focused on coaching skills and professional development
PATH Intl.	Therapeutic/adaptive riding	Certified Therapeutic Riding Instructor (CTRI) credential for equine-assisted services
British Horse Society (BHS)	International standard	Offers globally recognized instructor and trainer certifications

Additional Certification Programs

- **Equine Studies Institute (ESI)**
  - Offers online certifications for **Professional Horse Trainer**, **Riding Instructor**, and **Stable Manager**.
  - Flexible, course-based approach with certificates awarded per completed module.
- **British Horse Society (BHS)**
  - Internationally recognized qualifications for instructors and trainers.
  - Levels range from **Stage 1–5**, covering horse care, riding, coaching, and management.
  - Widely required in the UK and respected globally.
- **International Group for Equestrian Qualifications (IGEQ Passport)**
  - Provides a standardized international credential for riding instructors.
  - Helps professionals work across borders with recognized qualifications.
- **Federation Equestre Internationale (FEI) Coaching System**
  - Offers structured coaching courses worldwide.
  - Focuses on disciplines under FEI governance (dressage, jumping, eventing, endurance, etc.).
- **Specialized CHA Certifications** (beyond basic instructor levels):
  - **Trail Guide Certification**
  - **Vaulting Coach Certification**
  - **Driving Instructor/Driver Certification**
  - **Instructor of Riders with Disabilities Certification**
  - **Equine Facility Manager Certification**

All these certification programs are a terrific resource for properly qualifying instructors and trainers. These specialized programs have been made available for prospective trainers and instructors who may or may not have received a university or college education in an equine related discipline. When you carefully consider certification credentials, you come to the realization that while it does cost the candidate money, time, practice, and dedication, trainers and instructors are paid quite well for their time. The following is a general breakdown of trainer and instructor costs according to *Bay Area Equestrian Network* and *Great American Adventures:*

Riding Instructor Costs

- **Group lessons:** Around **$25–$40 per session**. These are more affordable since costs are shared among multiple students.
- **Private lessons:** Typically, **$50–$100 per hour**, depending on the instructor's certification, experience, and location.
- **Semi-private lessons:** Often fall in between, around **$40–$60 per hour**.
- **Regional variation:** Prices differ widely by state or country. For example, lessons in rural areas may be closer to $25, while urban centers or high-demand stables may charge $80–$100.

Horse Trainer Costs

- **Hourly lessons with a trainer:** Usually **$35–$75 per hour**, with private sessions averaging **$50 per hour**.
- **Full training programs:** A 30-day horse training package often costs **$3,000–$6,000**, depending on the trainer's reputation and the horse's needs.
- **Annual trainer income:** On average, horse trainers earn about **$33,943 per year** in the U.S., with hourly rates around **$16.32**. Top trainers can make significantly more.

Factors Affecting Price

- **Instructor/Trainer experience & certification** – Highly qualified professionals charge more.
- **Lesson type** – Group vs. private, English vs. Western riding styles.
- **Location** – Urban stables and competitive regions cost more than rural areas.
- **Additional expenses** – Gear, stable fees, horse boarding, and transportation can add to the total.

Certification is an asset to those who do the work and earn the credentials. Not only does it benefit them, but it is also an indication to horse owners that this person has undergone training to become a professional in the field. Always attempt to seek out a qualified professional trainer or instructor if possible. It will be beneficial to you and your horse.

What Should I Look for in a Trainer?

As you may have noticed, I have used the words *trainer* and *instructor* somewhat interchangeably and have done so for a purpose. For purposes of discussion and debate, one term and description coincide with the other in most cases.

It is very important that you be comfortable and confident with your trainer. It is also important to realize that you may use numerous trainers with your horse over time. Realize that this is not a disadvantage as more than one opinion and style can be advantageous to you and your horse—although consistency certainly matters. Think about it as if you were in school in your younger years. You progressed through all the grades and encountered numerous mentors and teachers. You had your favorites as well as those you just tolerated. You will find that your relationships with trainers are no different. You and your horse may connect with some, and there may be no connection at all with others. This is perfectly natural and to be expected.

Trainers are blessed with one fundamental trait that we all possess—an opinion. They develop their own style, even when employing standardized methods that they may learn in an equine certification program and practice their trade in hopes of finding the method that works universally. The reality is that you and your horse are both individuals. With that comes differing habits, physical abilities or constraints, and unique dispositions. Therefore, each client may be unique in some respects and typical of others. Many trainers have adopted or adapted their methods from other popular and effective trainers—some of whom may have taught or mentored them in the past. We all carry a piece of those who have influenced us through the years, and this is how knowledge and expertise is passed on to others.

So, what makes a trainer the right trainer? The answer will be different for each person and horse. At this point, let's develop a general criterion for all of us to use in the future. It may be of some help to you to have a useful acronym in mind when searching for the right trainer. The acronym that I would suggest is **PERISCOPE**. In and of itself, you can equate this acronym to your mission of setting your sights on making the right targeted decision.

P *Professional*

E *Enthusiastic*

R *Realistic*

I *Innovative*

S *Safety-oriented*

C *Certified*

O *Organized*

P *Patient*

E *Educated*

Let us now examine each term designated in the acronym and its relevance to your decision. *Professional* means that your trainer will conduct business ethically and will be trustworthy with you, your horse, and your time. *Enthusiastic* means that your trainer will always strive to exhibit a positive attitude and will make learning interesting and fun for you and your horse. *Realistic* means that your trainer will work within your latitude of abilities and not be overzealous in their expectations. *Innovative* refers to a trainer who is always searching to develop more effective methods. *Safety-oriented* means that your trainer will not violate the principles of safety and risk management at any time. *Certified* refers to a trainer who has invested their time and energy in obtaining credentials and qualifications for the benefit of riders and horses. *Organized* means that your trainer has a carefully crafted plan of development for the progress of you and your horse. *Patient* means that your trainer will not force you to initiate a command that triggers apprehension. *Educated* means that you expect your trainer to have devoted time and energy to educate him or herself in the discipline like any other professional who is paid for their time.

Hopefully this useful acronym will assist you in initially defining what qualities you are searching for in your prospective trainer. This will enable you to make a more intelligent decision while considering whether this person possesses these necessary qualities and attributes. It is very easy. At the very least, take sufficient time to fill in the blanks and make a solid choice that benefits you and your horse.

<u>Training Options</u>

As you may suspect, a rigorous training schedule can be time-consuming as well as expensive. Yet, I believe that it is a vital part of ownership that cannot be easily replaced. If you are considering a purchase, I would suggest that you plan to include training costs in your working budget. Unless you are an established rider or trainer yourself, it may be very difficult to implement an effective training plan for you and your horse. On the other hand, I have seen several horse owners who chose to train on their own. In most cases, this decision was not very effective because they lacked expertise. Naturally, your horse's use will dictate much of what may be needed in training. For example, a dressage horse is going to need much more training than a pleasure horse. Hence, the anticipated expense.

I have found that even the best riders will continue to engage with professional trainers in hopes of honing their skill level to even further heights. You will also find that even the most recognized trainers are constantly developing principles and methods to gain a competitive edge with which to educate riders and their horses.

There are several options when seeking a training program and an educator. You will find that programs are as diverse as the number of trainers available, and that the time, cost, and results will all differ.

There are three basic training arrangements that you'll find to be available for you as a new horse owner: the **onsite training program**, the **outside training program**, and the **appointment training program**. The onsite training program is designed for the traditional border. It is optionally included in a full-service stable facility agreement. This arrangement is typically utilized by those boarders with the financial capability and veracity to stick with the training schedule. The outside training program is designed for those riders that may not have the financial ability to invest in full-time onsite training but could travel to the trainer's facility. The appointment training program is one in which the student/owner has a trainer who makes farm calls for training. This program is often the costliest, as it requires travel by the trainer.

Many stable facilities have professional trainers on their staff to meet the needs of boarders first and outside riders as well. At a full-service facility, you may expect lessons, training, feeding, grooming, transportation and any other number of services to be included at one comprehensive price. Arrangements may also be available to modify the services based upon your need or level of participation. Understand that the amount of training and lessons can have a tremendous impact on your monthly costs. Geographic location may also impact pricing as well. It can be expensive, but you do receive many services and the full-time presence of your trainer being on staff. You may not possess the financial ability to afford a full-service facility, but that does not by any means exclude you or your horse from an education and professional instruction.

The late Gary Zook, a professional horse trainer from Flemington, NJ, developed an innovative training program for the outside rider that merits some discussion, and it may assist you in making a good decision if you are unable to afford a full-time facility. Gary was the 1982 winner of the first Adult Medal Finals National Championship and was a partner in his show stable, *River's Edge*.

According to his article *"Big Time Training on a Budget"* published by *Practical Horseman* in September of 1992, Gary started with a program that he defined as "a detailed way of planning and handling everything to do with the horse. I don't just teach writing—though that's an important piece. My away lessons and those [lessons] I teach at *River's Edge* for outside students who ship in also encompass tack, training schedules, stable management, shoeing, healthcare, and show turn-out—things my boarders get the benefit of without having to think about much."

Gary saw his local outside students once a week for lessons and charged approximately $50 per lesson at the time, depending on the length of travel. Between lessons, Gary talked with his students by phone, discussed progress and problems, and offered advice to either resolve the problem or lend support. Students also met Gary at shows approximately twice a month. He would charge $75 to $100 per student at that time, depending on the amount of time necessary for that student and his or her horse. During show season, Gary would also meet students at shows for lessons in his off time to keep students in tune. Gary stated that his approach gave him enough contact with his students to lay out a foundation, but the practice was left up to the student. While it is true that the student will be required to do more work for herself than the traditional boarder, she would get positive results with practice and contact with Gary.

Gary also believed in "introducing stable management skills" to his students "the minute I walk into a student's barn." He also took the time to evaluate feeding schedules and any health-related problems and made suggestions as to treatments and alternative therapies such as acupuncture or chiropractics. He also addressed the choice of tack from the outset so that there was no confusion over equipment. These suggestions were helpful to the outside student because he or she may have never been advised otherwise.

It is clear that if you can afford a full-service facility, you will reap the benefits. But if you cannot, you should not feel excluded. It is very possible to get positive results, especially since there are trainers like Gary Zook who try to accommodate outside students. In either case, you're sure to succeed if you invest the time and practice.

While the three aforementioned training options are the predominant choices, you will find that any arrangement is negotiable and can be customized to fit your needs. Many trainers or stable facilities will allow you to board your horse at that facility for a determined period specifically designated for training. That period may be anywhere from 30 to 90 days or longer, and the length of time for training is up to the two parties. Of course, you will be required to pay the trainer's fees, stable board, and any other agreed upon price for additional services. Once the training is complete, you simply move your horse back to his facility. This arrangement is ideal for off-season training or moving the horse out of an inclement climate temporarily.

What Should I Require for a Trainer?

The answer is simple: performance. You are paying the trainer to perform a specified service. Therefore, that trainer, whether nationally known or a local horseperson, is expected to live up to your expectations and meet his or her business obligations. Let's assume that you have scrutinized this person's qualifications and abilities and establish a working list of things to check.

1) Make sure that you are aware of the amount of time that your trainer will spend with your horse each day and how many days per week that he or she will be working. I suggest at least an hour a day, five days a week, with two days off for rest. Defer to the expertise of your trainer.

2) Ask for a written training plan that will be designed specifically for you and your horse. This plan should include goals to be attained and a pathway to achieving success for both of you.

3) Do your best to be present at every session, even if just to observe the trainer. If you are not welcome at a training session by your trainer, this would serve as a red flag to me. The curriculum should be geared toward you as the rider, and a trainer would be remiss not to include you. Of course, the situation may present itself in which your trainer will want to work solely with your horse, but you are encouraged to observe and make mental notes.

4) If you are sending your horse off property to a trainer that is located out of town, make sure that you have traveled to the facility to inspect safety conditions and general care standards. There are trainers with whom I would entrust my horse when I am not present, but it is best practice to be present. Sending your horse to training may be a difficult decision to make, although it may be very effective. Unfortunately, while a trainer may get the results that you want, you are not able to participate.

5) Make certain that your trainer is consistent. If you are scheduled for a thirty-day training period, specify that the horse will work five days with the weekend off. It is very important to your horse that he becomes familiar with his schedule and routine. You will find that the results will be more positive with consistency. Horses catch on quickly to routines.

6) Ascertain what *exactly* is included in training. You will need to know if lessons, showing and schooling at a show, and transportation are included in your training agreement.

7) It is a good idea to watch the prospective trainer in person to see whether he or she forces results from a horse and a rider. According to trainer Kit Young-Knox, trainer of Duce, the 1990 Grand Prix Horse of the Year, *"forcing a horse (or rider to) perform—even when he's not sure what's being asked of him—can create confusion and spawn resentment. Over time, it can obliterate a mount's trust in his rider."* I can personally attest to the obliteration of trust that Young-Knotts refers to in her statement. My horse, Rhythm King's first trainer, had an obvious problem with establishing dominance over whatever horse he was training. I personally witnessed many unnecessary and harsh corrections and conflicts that were instigated by an overly aggressive trainer. Finding the right trainer who can subtly control a

horse in a positive way is key. Training is a give and take situation that warrants patience on the part of the trainer and the rider. You will develop a partnership with your horse by gaining his trust and cooperation. Harsher methods are typically counterproductive and may be unacceptable to you as an owner.

8) Inquire with your trainer as to what training devices may be used in training your horse. If the trainer does use a device of any kind, make certain she explains its use and what benefit may be gained by employing the device. More traditional methods are used to gradually build specific muscles to promote ideal carriage. Some devices can interfere with natural development and cause the horse to carry himself in an inefficient manner.

9) Ask for a prospective training estimate so that you may plan a financial strategy for the present and future. In other words, try to calculate what it may cost to achieve your goal. If, for example, you wish to ride your horse at Dressage Level 1 and he is currently capable of a walk and trot, ask the trainer for a ballpark figure and time expectation that they anticipate achieving your goal. Understand that this will be sheer (but professional) speculation, but I believe that you will be better prepared if you attempt to calculate your investment.

10) As with any other business you conduct, insist that you and your trainer have a training agreement that has been reduced to writing. This contract will ensure that all agreed upon services are rendered as specified and that you are properly protected. Remember though, training is not an exact science. You and your trainer may make certain plans for you and your horse, but at the end of the training period, you or the horse may come up short of your expectations. On the contrary, you and he may exceed those expectations. All you can ask of a trainer is that they perform up to their standards and that they invest in the time and effort that you have asked for in your agreement. While there are certainly substandard trainers, I do believe that the vast majority will do their utmost to see that you succeed and get your money's worth. Trainers have a vested interest in successful riders and horses to bolster their professional reputation.

11) As we discussed previously, make sure that your trainer carries the proper insurance coverage applicable to his or her duties. As previously mentioned, a commercial liability or errors and emissions (E&O) policy would be

appropriate in this situation. I am confident that you understand the importance of proper insurance coverage, so just make certain that the trainer has it in place.

12) Lastly, make sure that your trainer is accessible to you if you have a problem. A good trainer and businessperson will be available to you if you have been or are presently a client. It is your option to keep your horse in training all year if you have the financial capability to do so, but if you train more intermittently, your trainer should still be reasonably accessible. It is important to realize, however, that professional trainers make their living training, and their time is worth that of any comparable professional. Thus, there is a reasonable limit and expectation of accessibility and free advice.

This twelve-point checklist should be of great assistance to you in qualifying a potential trainer. Choosing any professional can be quite cumbersome because so much is at stake. But if you use your best judgment and an established methodology of making an intelligent choice, your chances improve tremendously. Keep in mind that you may make the wrong choice. It happens. If you do find yourself in that predicament, you must have the resolve to terminate the relationship as amicably as possible. There is no shame in disagreeing with someone's methods or having a clash of personalities.

A Happy Camper

Believe me when I tell you that I have been through the training and instruction dilemma. It can be a very difficult process to evaluate and choose the right trainer as a new owner or the parent of a new rider. As I stated, it is not an exact science—especially since it is difficult to even identify a professional because of the lack of certification requirements. This has been the case for decades.

When Rhythm King came into my life, I was totally uneducated with regards to choosing and evaluating a trainer. Moreover, I was naive enough to accept nearly every bit of advice and "experience" expounded upon me. I can assure you that after my experience with my first trainer, I felt intellectually inadequate. I simply didn't know any better and lacked experience.

When you become a new owner and make that first purchase, I suppose that you feel numb for a while and tend to let your guard down. This is especially true if only deal with one person throughout the entirety of the transaction, choose to board your horse at their facility, and use that particular person for training. At that point, you have only experienced one point of view, which can be limited and quite persuasive. This was the case in my first experience.

The methods that were used to train my horse seemed unacceptable to me as an owner, but there existed several other problems that I might point out for your future reference. First, our trainer would not allow another trainer of my choice on his property. I found this to be problematic, because I suspected problems and wanted a second opinion. There were three reasons: first, I was concerned about the welfare of my horse and invested money in this project. Second, my horse was in constant distress and acting totally out of character in comparison to other horses. As I stated before, I was not aware that forcible means were counterproductive to my horse's development and conflicts seem normal according to this trainer. Third, the trainer conducted training outside of my presence at his request. These facts, along with innumerable other discovered problems, all made for a horrible experience.

The inherent problem with the difficulties I explained was that I simply didn't know better. While I feel that this is a poor excuse, it was nonetheless the case. At that point, I was faced with a decision—my horse was unhappy; I felt tremendous guilt, and I felt as if I would never correct the situation. There is hope, and you can do the right thing if you are resolved to not let the same thing happen twice.

I decided that after a year at the stable facility that I would seek out a more acceptable boarding situation and a competent professional trainer. This time, I did my due diligence and was much more intelligent and informed in my decision-making process. I employed many of the preliminary steps that I have expanded upon thus far to intelligently choose a stable facility that met my needs and those of Rhythm King. It was my experience that a kinder, gentler approach in conjunction with a more organized and scientific methodology of training brought results that I had never expected. He was then a happy camper, full of vigor, more rider-friendly, and in a much better mood.

As indicated, I have personally experienced the training dilemma, but I lived through it—just as you will. Hopefully, you will find success in employing the methods that I have described and will not be forced to make the same mistake that I and many before me made by no choice of their own. Remember that performance, consistency, reputation, and results are the keys to a successful trainer/rider/horse relationship. You and your horse's happiness depend on it.

The Ego Trip

To properly conclude this chapter, it is necessary to address one more aspect of training and instruction. This aspect of our discussion seems to be the less popular side of the business, but an aspect that can have a tremendous effect on you, the equine consumer.

Some business relationships were meant to last, and some were not. Simply because a business relationship ends, it does not necessarily indicate that you or the other party are unethical or mean people. Nonetheless, you should be insightful enough to realize that you may not agree with every method or opinion that is conveyed to you. More importantly, we hope that the other person—namely your trainer—has the same attitude and understanding. Unfortunately, this is not always the case and worth further examination.

Trainers are somewhat like beautiful horses. Once a horse reaches a certain level of beauty, they are not necessarily more beautiful than other horses, but just different. The same principle applies to trainers. Once a trainer reaches a certain level of expertise, they may not necessarily be better than the next excellent trainer, but just different. In other words, this is less of a competition and more of a quest for knowledge. And while a competitive spirit is healthy, there are trainers who take it to the extreme.

If you are attempting to select a professional trainer, there is one thing that should be clear in your mind: you should be certain that this person remembers who is employing them. If you do not agree with or understand a certain method, let the trainer know without hesitation. Finally, ask for an explanation of the method. Do not give any trainer *carte blanche* authority over your horse, regardless of their experience or credentials. You are paying for the training and that person resides within your service. Period.

Another important aspect of training that you need to address is whether your stable facility allows you to employ an outside trainer. Many do not. I feel this to be a red flag. As I said, not all business relationships are meant to last, but that should not mean that you should be penalized because only one trainer is permitted or available at a facility. Should you be forced to use a trainer with whom you have a personality conflict or disagreement over her methodology? Of course not, but you may find this unfortunate situation to be the case at many facilities. Regrettably, personal ego sometimes plays an important role in the minds of some "professionals." Here, we come to another crossroads concerning professionals. Let me be more concise.

I once had the displeasure of experiencing this attitude at a stable facility where Rhythm King was boarded. I made certain, upon review of the boarding contract, that if I was not satisfied with the facility trainer, I had the option of employing a trainer of my choice. My trainer would be permitted to train my horse at the facility, but I was responsible to notify the facility's trainer so that no conflict occurred regarding use of the facilities or equipment. I found this to be acceptable, and the facility owner stated that she did not like to do it, but she "had no choice." That was true; she really did not have a choice. However, when I opted to hire an outside trainer, there was resistance that made the decision unappealing to me and ultimately for the outside trainer. As a result, I chose to leave the facility. While it is true that I could have forced the issue, friction compromised the relationship. In hindsight, I should have interpreted her reluctance and resistance as a sign of poor business ethics.

Your trainer's opinion is worth much to you if you trust that person and confide in them for their support. However, their opinion is not the only one available. If your trainer is a true professional, he will readily admit that you may want to seek another opinion should you disagree with him. But if that person berates you for questioning them or their opinion, then you may have made a questionable choice. Remember, you are the owner of your horse and you alone will make the final decision on matters concerning his welfare. A true professional will invite you to seek out other opinions and will not be offended. This is the type of trainer you should seek out. If you sense any resistance to outside instruction or training in your initial conversation with a stable facility, my advice is to consider avoiding this facility for training.

Some of us have egos that make us competitive and make us strive for perfection. But in a profession where you are seeking professional advice and training, egos should not overwhelm proper decisions. Not only is it your money and time at stake, but also the welfare of your horse. Make sure that someone else's ego is not in any way destructive to your horse's promise or your potential?

Chapter Seven: The Pre-Purchase Exam

As you have learned thus far, there is much to know about equine ownership. From reading prior chapters, I am sure that it has become clear that there are several issues of which you should be aware before ever considering horse ownership. But if you have paid close attention to the details and have drawn some common sense conclusions of your own relating to financial impact, your ability as a rider, your level of commitment, and the inherent liability, you should now be ready to approach the essence of the purchase.

All the information (both facts and opinions) that I have related to you thus far should give you a strong foundation on which to build your purchase process. With that preliminary knowledge, we can now concentrate on the practical side of the purchase. Notwithstanding, all we have discussed so far is still of great importance and should not be easily forgotten. Although you are now getting closer than ever to actual ownership, remain cautious, calculated, and pragmatic.

In this chapter, we will discuss one of the most important aspects of a horse purchase known as the **Pre-Purchase Exam**. We will take a very close look at its impact on your decision and why it is so very important to include it as part of your purchase process. We will also discuss the pros and cons of having a pre-purchase exam and the potential danger of not committing to the exam itself. It is my hope that after reviewing this chapter, you will realize the importance of professional advice and the importance of drawing a conclusion based more upon fact and less upon opinion. The pre-purchase exam will often influence or dissuade you in making that final decision.

We will also be discussing the preliminary financial expenditures that I feel are necessary to ensure the success of your purchase. I do want to stress once again that your horse is an investment as well as a purchase. Therefore, it is not uncommon to have some related expenditures as part of the process. Of course, we must establish what expenditure is reasonable and customary. We will do this by considering your budget, monetary value of the purchase, and your connection to the horse.

You may also find that my suggested purchase process and methodology are somewhat different than the advice that you may read about in some horse-related periodicals. It is my hope that by the end of this chapter you will thoroughly understand why I recommend a slightly different approach from the norm and why it might work best for you.

The pre-purchase exam is a safety mechanism that you should employ prior to your final purchase. This mechanism is multifaceted in purpose as it serves many functions in the pre-purchase process that are of importance to you as a potential buyer.

The pre-purchase exam is performed with the purpose of providing you with preliminary information about the horse's health, physical abilities, abnormalities, or handicaps that may affect his performance or health then or in the future. With the results of the pre-purchase exam in hand, you will be better able to make a more informed and intelligent decision regarding purchase or the avoidance thereof. Without this information, you could potentially be asking for difficulties from the outset. It is our hope, of course, that your prospect will pass the exam with flying colors, but "perfection" can be costly.

There are some preliminary steps that I suggest before you choose to have a pre-purchase exam performed—the most important of which is to learn something about the history of your prospect. If the horse is registered, you should ask the breeder or seller to review papers and pedigrees. If this information is not available, I would insist (if possible) that it be made available before you consider your purchase. With this information, you now have the ability to research bloodlines and relatives and to evaluate any inherited or common health problems seen within that specific bloodline.

Another aspect of a horse's history that should be evaluated is any prior training. Attempt to find out who broke the horse and the names of any trainers who worked with the animal prior to your consideration for purchase. If it is possible to reach the trainers, I would suggest that you ask a number of questions—some of which are: Did you train the horse aggressively? Did the horse have any lameness or injury problems while in your care? What was the horse's disposition while in training? Did he suffer any injuries from trailer accidents? Does he have any bad habits or vices? What devices, if any, did you use during your training? Are you a Western or English trainer? These are a few pertinent questions that you may want to have answered for your own peace of mind and research. Knowing the horse's background may provide an edge in the decision-making process.

Yet another invaluable source of pre-purchase information is the evaluation of prior medical records. These records should be made available to you. I would examine them carefully and make notations of any condition or injury that concerns you. Moreover, it is a great idea to have an equine practitioner examine the records and provide a professional opinion as to the horse's present and future soundness. Any responsible owner retains these records and should have no problem sharing them to you prior to purchase. What if the horse Is not registered? What if you cannot locate prior owners or trainers? What if he has no notable prior training? If these conditions exist, then you must consider costs, physical evaluation, and your personal connection with the horse and do the best you can with little preliminary information.

First and foremost, you need to determine the requisite purpose for your intended horse ownership. This will determine how specific your purchase criteria must be as it relates to specific breeds, bloodlines, and pedigree. Many fantastic horse/owner relationships started with a horse that was in no way particularly outstanding. A champion pedigree may mean a great deal to some but may be somewhat meaningless to others. The most important thing in horse ownership is your connection with him and the joy that he brings. Naturally, some horse buyers are much more utilitarian in purpose—which is fine and understandable—but it is not the prerequisite for everyone. Some otherwise "average" horses have become quite accomplished over the years without an outstanding pedigree. He may live up to every expectation you ever had and more if given the opportunity.

Screening a Prospect

Many publications related to the horse industry have published very informative articles concerning pre-purchase exams. Some of these articles are of some length and of great detail. An attempt to explain how to perform a successful and comprehensive pre-purchase exam.

I have read and reviewed many such articles in numerous publications and found them to be very informative and well-written. Unfortunately, if you are a potential new owner, it is somewhat unrealistic to expect you to understand the concept, terminology, and practical application of a pre-purchase exam. Terms such as *flexion test, ground check, withers, and stifle* will likely seem foreign to you unless you have been around horses for some time. The fact is that you are probably not qualified to conduct a formal pre-purchase exam and draw practical conclusions simply based upon your lack of experience.

The best advice is to turn to an experienced, educated professional who can conduct a thorough and effective pre-purchase exam as well as offer their professional opinion and guidance regarding your potential purchase. While I have seen many horses purchased without pre-purchase evaluations without incident, the converse can be quite costly if you rely on yourself or self-acclaimed "professional". The very best resource that you have for conducting an effective pre-purchase exam and equipping yourself with the best information possible in making your decision is your qualified equine practitioner. Additionally, it may even be valuable to include a reputable trainer in the process. Obviously, nothing is guaranteed in animal ownership of any kind, but consulting these professionals will increase your chances of success.

You may recall our discussion back in Chapter Two regarding the *trial lease*. My suggestion is that before you commit to a formal pre-purchase evaluation, hiring your professionals, and considering a purchase, you initiate a trial lease of your prospect so that you can personally acquaint yourself with her. This will give you a great opportunity to learn about her habits and physical capabilities, give you time to interact with her, and see if the connection exists. Using the trial lease involves limited commitment on your part and will give you considerable information that cannot be obtained through a one-hour pre-purchase evaluation. Furthermore, this will enable you to employ the services of your trainer to spend time with you and the horse assessing her assets and attributes. In this way, you are getting an extended look at the horse on a day-to-day basis—which will be just as valuable as the pre-purchase exam itself.

Taking time to personally evaluate the horse on your own and with your trainer also gives you a chance to examine the movements of the horse. This is essential because you will be able to bring specific points of concern to the attention of the equine practitioner at the pre-purchase exam. Taking the time to do this may make you aware of the fact that "she does not like to turn left" or "she flinches when I mount." This feedback will be of great value to you, your equine practitioner, and the horse and will help ensure an informed decision-making process.

Including Your Equine Practitioner

As you may have guessed, a thorough pre-purchase exam should be performed by your qualified equine practitioner. As we discussed in Chapter 4, this is the person who has dedicated many years of their life and education to veterinary medical training and has gained the qualifications and credentials to evaluate your horse.

In my eyes, any opinion is secondary to that of your equine practitioner. Some less-experienced horse buyers often rely on a trainer or buyer agent to offer a final opinion concerning purchase but note that these folks are usually paid a fee or commission. While this is not unethical, that person does have a monetary incentive. Your equine practitioner will certainly charge a fee for his or her services but will likely offer the most unbiased opinion.

You should expect your equine practitioner to inform you of any existing abnormalities or potential physical problems that may arise out of your horse's intended use. He or she will perform a number of tests, including but not limited to: examining eyes for cataracts or any old scars or past inflammation, checking the head for unusual lumps or tumors, checking the sinuses, checking the heart rate for any unusual sounds on both sides, palpating the back and checking the spine, listening to the lungs and respiratory system, performing an endoscopic exam looking for blockages or sores in the airway, checking the soft tissue and joints of the legs for abnormalities, checking the stifle, checking the teeth, and thoroughly examining each foot.

In addition to the aforementioned points of examination, it is valuable to request a few other tests. I would highly suggest that x-rays be part of your pre-purchase examination. The most experienced veterinarians can sometimes miss existing conditions or past damage in an external examination. However, with x-rays, you can increase your chances of accuracy dramatically. Without x-rays, you leave yourself vulnerable to future problems that may have otherwise been avoided or treated. Remember, veterinarians are people too and can sometimes overlook an issue that they cannot see. I have seen hasty decisions made on the part of otherwise competent equine practitioners. Had x-rays been taken, the owner would have saved time and money, and the horse would not have had to endure wasted or ineffective treatment.

Many horse sales take place without the use of x-rays. I see this practice as unwise. Many "professionals" and private individuals will sell horses with undisclosed pre-existing conditions that x-rays would have surely exposed. An unethical seller counts on your lack of experience and knowledge to make a sale. Don't let your lack of thoroughness inhibit what should be an enjoyable experience. Although x-rays are an extra expense in the pre-purchase examination, they are invaluable and can be done right on site with your veterinarian's portable equipment.

Physical performance testing should also be part of your pre-purchase regimen. Your veterinarian will probably ask you to walk and trot the horse to visually search for any external signs of lameness. See to it that you are asked to do this on hard *and* soft surfaces, as hard surfaces tend to show signs of lameness more easily. I recall that before I decided to shoe Rhythm King (on the advice of our veterinarian) he appeared to move fine on grass, a soft surface, but when asked to trot on a hard sand driveway, we found that he was tender in the feet and showed some discomfort. Your equine practitioner will likely also ask you to lunge the horse in circles to again visually examine the horse's movement. You should also be prepared to ride the horse for the veterinarian or request that a potential trainer or friend do this in your place. Thus, it is important that you have made a decision regarding his intended use so that he can be tested for that particular purpose. In other words, if the horse is going to jump, it is a good idea that the veterinarian evaluates his ability and form in that activity to search for any physical flaws while jumping.

Another test that should be performed is a **ground check**. Your veterinarian will check the horse's general appearance and observe his movements and general habits. Examination will also be done of the teeth, skin, jaws, hooves, tail, gums, and flank movement to measure respiratory rate and pattern.

Lastly, your equine practitioner will also perform **joint-flexion tests.** Your vet will flex certain joints for a period of a minute or so and will then release them. This method will aggravate any soreness, thus informing the veterinarian that there may be a problem. This test should also be done on ankles, knees, stifles, and hocks. This test will indicate a normal range of motion and any present lameness. This is also a great way to test joints naturally. After you have become more acquainted with handling your horse, you may be able to be somewhat effective with this test, yourself, in the future. It can be helpful for you in identifying minor lameness problems, although diagnosing precisely where the problem lies is much more difficult for an amateur. Notwithstanding, this can help you convey a prospective issue of concern to your equine practitioner.

After the pre-purchase examination is completed, make certain that your equine practitioner has accurately recorded all information on a pre-purchase exam form. This form should have basic information including the name of the horse, age, sex, color, breed, markings, prospective use, prospective buyer's name, seller's name, and a record of all findings. If additional tests, lab work, or X-rays are taken and need to be evaluated later, you will receive a copy of those findings. Again, it is very important that you have your final choice of horse narrowed down if possible. Pre-purchase exams and their cost is typically the sole responsibility of the potential buyer.

The following equine pre-purchase exam (PPE) menu from *Piedmont Equine Practice* in Virginia is an example of the anticipated costs you may incur:

Farm Call Fee $80 to $100 (depending on location)

Hospital Admission Fee $47

PPE on Farm and Clinic $575
Includes physical exam, eyes, heart, respiratory, temperature, palpation of limbs and hoof tester exam, trotting in hand, lunging, and observation under saddle. Full flexions are done on all 4 limbs.

Sedation $30

Optional Bloodwork

CBC/Chemistry/Fibrinogen $148.50
Coggins: Rushed – $65.50, Standard – $43.50
Drug Screen –

> Center for Toxicology Services Basic Drug Screen + Fedex $431
> Center for Toxicology Services Plus Firocoxib +Fedex $710.50
> Center for Toxicology Services Elisa Reserpine ONLY $128 +Fedex

Antech Domplete Drug Screen (Antech Diagnostics) $525.82
Interstate Health Certificate (if necessary) $47.50
Upper respiratory tract video scoping $210
Ultrasound – reproductive $87.50
Ultrasound – limb $278.50

Radiographs and Other Services
There is a radiology set-up fee of $65 at Farm Call appointments

Sedation $30.00 plus the price of administered medications

PPE Extremities package – $1390
36 views including 8 front feet, 10 fetlock, 4 hind fetlock, 8 hock, 6 stifle. Limited substitutions allowed at the discretion of the examining veterinarian. Additional extremity images are $65/view.

PPE Extremities and Back – $1585
41 views including the extremity package plus three views of the dorsal spinous processes and 2 of the vertebral bodies.

PPE Extremities and Neck – $1620
extremities package plus 5 lateral views of the neck.

PPE Extremities, Neck, Back – $1815
extremities package plus neck package plus back package.

Single radiographs are $65 per view – average per joint is 4 views

Upper respiratory tract video scoping $210

Ultrasound – reproductive $87.50

Ultrasound – limb $278.50

As you can see, even the basic pre-purchase exam is quite expensive notwithstanding all the add-ons that are available. Generally, it is a risk versus return scenario mainly being determined by the monetary value/price of the horse. Naturally, a potential buyer looking at a $100,000 horse should expect to invest $2500 in a thorough pre-purchase exam, but what about the $3000 horse you are considering? In my opinion, a pre-purchase exam—even a basic (PPE)---is worth the cost for some peace-of-mind and the well-being of your new friend. In the end, you will have to be the judge.

Draw the Line

When is a pre-purchase exam simply not worth the money? There are isolated cases in which you might opt for a basic exam or forgo the exam altogether. If you are planning to purchase a horse that is well into adulthood and plan to use the horse simply for pleasure or trail riding, you may decide against the pre-purchase exam simply based upon the price of the horse and its intended use. I doubt that any horse is perfect, but you can be relatively sure that an older horse has the common natural problems related to age and possibly his former use. But if he or she appears to be generally sound and has no otherwise obvious problems, you may opt to make the purchase without the exam. I cannot say that I disagree in this instance but would still recommend a general health exam just to protect his well-being and to make yourself aware of his current state of health.

The bottom line is that it is always helpful to be aware and prepared concerning the health of your horse—or any animal for that matter. Even in a case where you acquire a horse at no cost to you, such as a rescue situation, a veterinary evaluation and health check is always recommended.

The Veterinarian's Caution

The following is a 2024 revised statement courtesy of *American Association of Equine Practitioners* concerning their "Guidelines for Reporting Purchase Examinations":

These guidelines are to provide a framework to aid the examining veterinarian during a purchase exam; however, it is the buyer's responsibility to determine if the horse is suitable for their intended use. These guidelines are neither designed for nor intended to cover any examinations other than purchase examinations (e.g., limited examinations at auction sales and other special purchase examinations, such as lameness, endoscopic, ophthalmic, radiographic, reproductive examinations, etc.). While compliance with all of the following guidelines helps to ensure a properly reported purchase examination, it remains the veterinarian's sole responsibility to determine the extent and depth of each examination. The AAEP recognizes that for practical reasons, not all examinations permit or require veterinarians to adhere to each of the following guidelines.

1. All reports should be included in the medical record.
2. The report should contain:
   1. A description of the horse with sufficient specificity to fully identify it.
   2. The time, date, and place of the examination.

3. The name and address of parties involved with the examination (buyer, seller, agent, witness, etc.).
4. All abnormal or undesirable findings discovered during the examination and give their qualified opinions as to the significance of these findings.

3. The veterinarian should make no determination and express no opinions as to the suitability of the animal for the purpose intended. This issue is a business judgment that is solely the responsibility of the buyer that they should make on the basis of a variety of factors, only one of which is the report provided by the veterinarian.

4. The veterinarian should record and retain in the medical record a detailed description and findings of all the procedures performed in connection with the purchase examination.

5. The veterinarian should record any recommendations expressed to the buyer with specific references to tests (X-rays, endoscopy, blood, drug, EKG, rectal, nerve blocks, laboratory studies, etc.) that were recommended but not performed on the horse at the request of the buyer.

6. A copy of the report and all documents relevant to the examination should be retained by the veterinarian for years not less than the statute of limitations applicable for the state in which the service was rendered. Local legal counsel can provide advice as to the appropriate period of retention.

Recommendations for Purchase Exams at Public Auction

- Radiographic interpretation for potential buyers should be performed by a veterinarian retained to represent that buyer's personal interest with their particular needs and level of risk tolerance in mind.
- Use of radiographic reports composed by the sellers' veterinarian for proposed buyers has the potential to jeopardize all parties involved. The buyer may not be represented adequately, the seller incurs greater risk by potentially misrepresenting the horse and the veterinarian does not have the opportunity to explain his/her findings and their relevance to resale or training, in their opinion.
- Veterinarians are encouraged to report all radiographic findings when interpreting radiographs for either the seller or buyer at public auction, with particular emphasis on those areas where pathology would commonly occur.

- Modifying or altering radiographic reports, including deleting findings by either the veterinarian or anyone with access to the report, so that they might be used as a positive marketing tool in the auction venue is considered unethical and fraudulent.
- Veterinarians with ownership in horses being presented for public auction should avoid being involved in the representation of those horses to potential buyers including, but not limited to, performing a radiographic or endoscopic assessment.
- Veterinarians involved in performing radiographic examinations on horses for sale at public auction should strive to provide optimum radiographic quality with respect to proper positioning and appropriate exposure of all required views to ensure accurate and reliable determinations of findings.

Radiographs – Custody and Distribution

The AAEP recommends the retention of all radiographs in an archiving system for a period of three years. The AAEP and AVMA consider this essential for protection against litigation. The assertion of legal precedent is that radiographs are the property of the veterinarians who produced them, and only the information interpreted from the radiograph is the property of the client. The radiographs can be forwarded electronically for distribution to the radiographic repository at public auction houses, as well as for referrals and consultations. They should be released upon the request of the owner or the owner's agent.

Revised by AAEP board of directors in 2024.

As you can see, this is a strong statement by the AAEP regarding their guidelines as they relate to purchase exams. Naturally, you are relying on your equine practitioner for advice and guidance, but you must realistically keep in mind that your equine practitioner does have liability exposure if he/she provides direct advice as to whether you should buy or pass on that particular horse. Jeffrey Witwer, DVM of the *Delaware Equine Center* in Pennsylvania stated that, "litigation is probably the main reason pre-purchase reports remain so non-committal - the less judgmental you are, the less likely you are to be sued by an irate buyer."

It is very important to realize that you will ultimately make the decision to purchase or not, and the decision should not be left up to the equine practitioner. The equine practitioner's only purpose in the pre-purchase stage is to perform a thorough veterinary exam at your direction and at your cost. With the veterinarian's findings, you are then left with the final decision to make the purchase or to opt out. You are also left with the task of evaluating all positive and negative factors and deciding whether you will accept the findings and make the purchase. In other words, it is a *buyer-beware* situation, and the final choice is solely up to you.

In the final analysis, be aware that while there are professionals like equine practitioners, trainers, breeders, other riders, and your equine attorney who are there to guide you, ultimately you are charged with making the final decisions. And don't forget that exams and advice will never replace your connection with a horse. If *you* feel good about it, make your decision with confidence either way.

Chapter Eight: Understanding Equine Law

All the chapters within this book are of great importance to you as a potential buyer and new owner. But of all the chapters within this book, this chapter is one of the most important. I do feel it incumbent upon me to make the disclosure that I am not an attorney, and I am not attempting to provide you with direct legal advice. Always consult a licensed and qualified attorney for legal advice. But it is important to share what I have learned about the very specialized field of equine law and how it may affect horse owners like you and me.

While doing my research for this book, I came to find out that one of the most specialized areas of legal practice was that of equine law. With equine law being so specialized, most consumers are likely not aware of laws and prior decisions that may soon affect you while dealing with the equine industry. This fact can leave you vulnerable in attempting to make decisions that may not be within your best interest or the best interest of your horse. Furthermore, you're left at a decisive disadvantage, because so few legal professionals and laypersons are cognizant of laws pertaining to the equine industry. This can be a hard pill to swallow if faced with an adverse situation.

According to the *Martindale-Avvo Network,* there are 807 attorneys and 741 law firms across 1661 locations in the United States that actively practice equine law, although many lawyers who are listed to practice equine law also practice in other areas such as contracts, liability, real estate, agriculture or sports law. The actual number of lawyers who practice primarily or exclusively in equine law is likely much smaller. Equine law is considered a "boutique practice area, often concentrated in states with large horse industries (KY, FL, TX, CA, CO, VA)."

If you are presented with a situation that requires the expertise of an equine law attorney, it is advisable to consult a database like *Lawyers.com* to seek out the nearest professional for consultation. Oftentimes, lawyers are licensed to practice in multiple jurisdictions and may be able to help. Typically, the most effective way of dealing with prospective legal issues is to have counsel in place or in mind prior to ever having a problem—which we hope never materializes.

For most horse owners, the closest you will ever come to needing legal advice is when signing a contract such as a boarding or lease agreement. The truth is that most general legal practitioners are fully qualified to review and advise you on these matters. Keep in mind that chances are high that any contract you sign as it relates to the equine business was likely prepared by a lawyer. Thus, it is good practice to have your lawyer review those contracts on your behalf. In my opinion, it is worth the consultation fee to have your lawyer's advice and input. In this way, you protect your interests and those of your horse.

Choosing an Attorney

If you are faced with a legal situation that potentially requires an equine law specialist, there is a sample list of roughly one-hundred practitioners listed in Appendix A.

When seeking an attorney, you'll generally employ the same criteria that was used in seeking an equine practitioner. It is always helpful to see if you have common ground with an attorney and that you feel comfortable with them personally. It is always advisable to have an attorney in mind *prior* to having a problem rather than scrambling to seek representation after the fact. The process can be as simple as calling an attorney's office and speaking to a paralegal who can give you the attorney's background and other basic information and letting the office know that you intend to contact them in the event that you have any legal issues related to their equine specialization. It is simply a matter of being prepared.

Another reason to address legal representation prior to a legal event is that obtaining representation is not always automatic. Unfortunately, many lawyers may be unsympathetic, too busy, or uninterested in your situation. Lawyers vet potential cases and make determinant judgements based upon their instincts and methodologies. In other words, they are not required to take your case.

Generally, attorneys who do the basics like return your calls or emails, take adequate time to explain points relative to your situation, and display a personable and professional attitude are the professionals whom you should seek out. The fact is that many law offices don't do the basics very well, which can leave you frustrated and anxious about finding someone to advocate on your behalf.

One of the more important aspects of choosing an equine law specialist is asking them about their experience in equine law. I once contacted an "equine" attorney because he had previously represented the State Horse Council. When I inquired about his past experience in equine cases, he advised me that he had once handled a case in which a barn had been destroyed by a fire. This was the extent of his expertise in equine law, at which time I deemed him not to have the expertise necessary. Although he seemed like a fine person, I found it necessary to seek out an attorney who had the necessary and relevant experience to best represent me. Again, all situations and cases are different. Many matters like stable agreements, lease agreements, and personal injury can be handled by a general practitioner but leave equine-specific matters to an attorney who has demonstrated competence in equine law matters.

Lastly, visit your county Clerk of Court website online to access public records involving your potential equine law specialist. This search may require you to visit numerous websites, but public information is available in which you can identify specific court actions in which your potential attorney was/is involved, often the applicable court documents, and the disposition of those cases. This is a great way to see how successful your potential lawyer has been in court advocating for his/her clients. Another trusted source of information is the applicable state bar association. You will be able to research if he/she is in good standing with the bar and to see if any formal complaints are pending.

In General

As a prospective horse owner, you've probably not even considered your legal position in that capacity. Don't feel bad because it is likely that most people have not given the matter much consideration either. It is also likely that legal issues are the furthest thing from your mind since you are so anxious to become a first-time horse owner. I can personally relate to that feeling but let me make clear that you should have a conscious understanding of your rights and responsibilities before entering horse ownership for the sake of your horse, yourself, and those around you.

I think that you would be quite surprised at how few laws are actually in place specifically geared toward the equine consumer. As I stated in Chapter Three, the equine industry generates a considerable portion of the gross national product, and it is obvious that without the equine consumer, this considerable portion of the economy would suffer. Yet you will find that most equine laws are legislated with only the equine professional/sponsor in mind. In this case, I am referring to stable owners, breeders, etc. On the judicial scale of justice, the consumer is not well-represented.

Most laws that have been legislated with regards to the equine industry have been enacted so that the industry itself may thrive. Laws pertaining to commercial liability matters have been given great consideration along with laws that protect equine sponsors and equine facilities. While it is a positive step for laws to be legislated to protect the industry and its sponsors, the consumer has been somewhat forgotten and often misused.

While it seems clear that less governmental intervention is sometimes best, there are instances in which regulation can be healthy and necessary. In an industry where so much of what is taught, instructed, and expounded upon is solely based upon opinion (qualified or not) it seems remiss to allow self-described "professionals" the ability to grant themselves an uncontested fiat of authority. It is also often the case that an inexperienced person like a new horse owner is taken advantage of because there are no concrete standards by which to measure a professional's level of expertise. When this becomes the case, you have very little recourse and no chance of intervention by a common authority, short of a civil lawsuit, to resolve what may be a legitimate grievance.

As is often the case in situations where there are no regulatory mechanisms on which to fall back, the vast majority of "professionals" resist any and all regulations, controls, or licensure. This has been the case for decades despite periodic attempts to invoke reasonable legislative or licensure requirements. The resistance seems to be a result of fear of any infringement upon "professionals" that might otherwise require them to verify an actual professional certification, license, or status as it relates to their professional credentials.

According to the *Michigan Farm News* in a 2023 study released in 2025, equine consumers spend as much as $177 billion each year in support of the equine industry. This fact should be acknowledged rather than dismissed by the hierarchy of the industry. If given the opportunity, equine consumers should continue to insist that reasonable but proper legislation and licensure be considered for the benefit of the consumer and their horses. It is clear that some compromise should be reached between the two entities, but the average horse owner simply may not realize that any problem exists until a problem arises between them and the professional.

There should be one parallel goal between equine professionals/sponsors and horse owners: to create and maintain a fair and just situation and relationship for both sides of the industry in order that the industry itself may thrive.

Stable Laws

Laws that apply to a stable facility are generally contractual in nature, although your state may have more concise statutes that relate specifically to stable facilities.

For example, in the State of South Carolina Code of Laws the word *"stable"* is only mentioned once. This particular law was in regards to an **agister's lien** which grants *"a stable owner or kennel keeper to have a lien upon any horse or dog which is left with him for upkeep, rest, and training until the cost of upkeep, rest, or training has been paid by the owner of the horse or dog. If the owner of the horse or dog has not paid the upkeep, rest, or training of the horse or dog after actual notice of the lien within sixty days of such notice, the stable or kennel keeper may sell the horse or dog."*

As we discussed in Chapter Five, you will expect that certain functions will be performed by the stable facility at which you board your horse. Hopefully you were presented with a formal contract that has been reviewed by legal counsel and agreed upon by you and the facility. Within this contract, you have clearly defined all requirements that you may have established and any contingencies that will nullify the contract if the facility does not perform its duties to your contract's satisfaction. The problem is that many facilities and barn managers have the attitude that *"if you don't like the terms of our contract, don't board here."* This is just a harsh reality in some cases. What's worse is that stable facilities are typically not terribly easy to come by; they may be limited in number, availability, or price.

If you are in a situation where keeping your horse on your property is not possible, do your best to find the most suitable situation for you and your horse at a stable facility that meets your needs and price point. I have seen so many situations in which conflicts arose at barns that were untenable and resulted in disputes, separations, and legal disputes. Just be aware that the horse community can be a bit cliquish in nature, so always have a secondary plan of action.

Sponsor Immunity

While equine activity is one of relaxation, challenges, and enjoyment, it is also one of inherent dangers. This fact should not necessarily discourage you from participating, but it should prompt you to exercise caution, safety, and prevention to mitigate as much risk as possible to you and others around you.

As in many other facets of life and activity, there exists a certain factor of liability that can fall upon someone's shoulders in the event of an accident or negligent act. Of course, no one looks forward to filing a lawsuit and being faced with the stress and expense of legal action, but our civil law system is set up so that a person may exercise an avenue of recourse and recover damages if it can be proven that another party was at fault. That is our legal remedy.

The issue of the utmost concern to professionals and sponsors within the equine industry is that of liability. This concern is well-founded and should be a priority on the list of any instructor, stable facility owner, trainer, barn manager, and any other person directly connected to equine activity. In fact, liability should concern any business owner, homeowner, or professional. Liability is part of the cost of doing business and is part of the world that we live in today.

Without question, there are frivolous lawsuits that clog our courts daily. Some of these lawsuits are unnecessary, some are fraudulent, and some are brought forth without any grounds whatsoever. However, there are many cases that have the merit to be litigated, and it is the right of the victim to be awarded damages if negligence or some other breach is proven in a court of law. This principle is fair and just when administered properly in civil court.

In Chapter Three, we discussed the importance of proper insurance coverage and have reiterated that fact throughout the entirety of this book. Why? The reason is that it is our responsibility to ourselves, our horse, and others around us to have the proper liability coverage in place in case of an accident or damage to property. This seems simple enough, and the cost is relatively modest. The problem is whether we are truly protected or not. In some cases, while you may be under the assumption that you would be protected from someone else's liability coverage, you may not be protected at all.

The equine industry has taken steps over the years to curb its level of liability with regards to a professional or sponsor's responsibility to a participant. In other words, legislation has been implemented by your state government that limits a professional or sponsor's liability should you become injured. How can that be? Equine professionals and sponsors have lobbied state governments and convinced legislators that they should not be held liable if you are injured or killed due to the inherent danger of equine activity.

According to the *Animal Legal and Historical Center* at *Michigan State University,* "Forty-eight states have enacted laws which limit the liability of equine sponsors and professionals, veterinarians, or others, for the injury or death of a participant as a result of, or due to the inherent risk of equine activity or agricultural tourism activities. These state statutes also provide the duties of equine activity participants. However, many statutes also provide exceptions for which the immunity of limited liability may not apply. Two states do not have any laws regarding equine activity liability (California and Maryland)."

Equine liability immunity laws provide significant benefits to sponsors and professionals by reducing the legal risks associated with the inherently unpredictable nature of horses. These statutes recognize that equine activities carry unavoidable dangers—such as sudden movements, environmental hazards, or the natural behavior of animals—that cannot be fully controlled even by experienced handlers. By shielding professionals and event organizers from lawsuits tied to these inherent risks, the laws create a more stable environment for equine businesses to operate. This protection encourages stables, riding schools, and event sponsors to continue offering services without the constant fear of crippling litigation, which in turn supports the growth of the equine industry as a whole.

Beyond reducing liability exposure, these laws also help equine professionals manage costs and maintain accessibility for participants. Insurance premiums for equine businesses are often lower when liability protections are in place, making it more affordable to run riding programs, host competitions, or sponsor events. The statutes also promote transparency by requiring warning signs and contractual language that inform participants of the risks they assume, fostering a culture of shared responsibility. This balance—protecting professionals while ensuring riders understand the dangers—allows equine activities to remain viable, affordable, and widely available, benefiting both providers and the communities they serve.

Equine liability immunity laws are considered reasonable and customary in many respects because they acknowledge the inherent risks of working with horses—animals that can be unpredictable despite the best training and care. Just as participants in skiing or other adventure sports accept certain dangers, riders and spectators at equine events are expected to recognize that accidents may occur even when professionals act responsibly. These statutes help balance the relationship between equine providers and participants by ensuring that professionals are not unfairly penalized for risks that cannot be eliminated, thereby allowing the industry to function without constant fear of litigation.

At the same time, some portions of these laws may feel less fair to participants, particularly when they seem to limit avenues for compensation after an injury. For example, broad immunity provisions can appear to favor equine businesses by shifting much of the burden of risk onto riders, even though participants may not fully appreciate the dangers involved. Critics argue that this imbalance can discourage accountability, especially if professionals rely too heavily on statutory protections rather than maintaining rigorous safety standards. From the participant's perspective, the laws can sometimes feel like a barrier to justice when harm occurs.

However, immunity laws are not absolute shields, and participants still retain legal recourse in specific circumstances. Most statutes carve out exceptions for negligence, reckless behavior, or failure to comply with statutory requirements such as posting warning signs or providing properly maintained equipment. If a professional knowingly provides unsafe tack, misrepresents a horse's temperament, or ignores a rider's skill level, liability can still attach. These exceptions ensure that while equine sponsors and professionals are protected from lawsuits over unavoidable risks, they remain accountable for preventable harm. In this way, the laws strike a balance between protecting the industry and preserving participants' rights to seek justice when genuine negligence occurs.

For equine participants, understanding your home state's equine liability immunity laws is essential because these statutes directly affect your rights and responsibilities. Each state has its own version of the law, with specific language, exceptions, and requirements such as posting warning signs or including statutory wording in contracts. By familiarizing yourself with these rules, you can better appreciate the risks and recognize the circumstances under which you may still have legal recourse. This knowledge empowers you to make informed decisions about the activities and the protections you expect from equine professionals.

Maintaining personal insurance coverage is another critical safeguard. Even with immunity laws in place, accidents can result in medical expenses, lost wages, or other financial burdens. Personal health or accident insurance ensures that participants are not left vulnerable if an injury occurs, especially in situations where liability cannot be assigned to the equine professional. Supplemental policies, such as equine activity insurance or liability coverage for horse owners, can provide additional peace of mind by filling gaps that general health insurance may not cover.

Finally, having access to a competent equine law specialist can make a significant difference when disputes arise. These attorneys understand the nuances of equine liability statutes and can advise you on whether a claim is viable under the exceptions carved out in the law. They can also help interpret contracts, waivers, and signage requirements to ensure participants are not unknowingly forfeiting rights. By combining legal awareness, personal insurance, and professional guidance, you can protect yourself while still enjoying the benefits and excitement of equine activities.

Legal Releases

Another element of the equine ownership process that will close your path is a **Legal Release**. This document is a written instrument of conveyance that is most often constructed and drawn by an attorney and presented to you by an equine professional, sponsor, trainer, stable facility, or riding club for your review and signature. This document is a written agreement in which a participant acknowledges the inherent risks of equine activities and agrees not to hold the professional, sponsor, or facility legally responsible for injuries, damages, or losses that may occur during participation. In essence, it is a contract designed to shift responsibility for those risks from the provider to the participant.

It is solely your choice whether to agree to the outlined terms and sign the release, but be aware that the professional, sponsor, or facility will likely make your participation contingent upon signing the document. These instruments typically include the following key elements:

Assumption of risk: The participant affirms that they understand horses are unpredictable, and that accidents may occur despite reasonable care and practice.

Waiver of liability: The participant agrees to waive their right to sue the equine professional or sponsor for injuries arising from inherent risks and equine activity.

Indemnification clause: In some cases, the participant agrees to reimburse the provider for costs if a claim is brought against them.

Compliance with state law: Many states with equine liability statutes require specific language or warnings to be included in the release for it to be enforceable.

Releases signed by equine participants are valuable tools for professionals and sponsors, but they are not foolproof. Courts generally uphold these agreements when they clearly outline the inherent risks of equine activities and demonstrate that the participant knowingly accepted those risks. However, a release cannot shield a provider from every possible claim of harm or negligence. If the language is overly broad, ambiguous, or fails to comply with state-specific statutory requirements, a judge may determine that the release is unenforceable. This means that while releases provide strong protection against lawsuits tied to inherent risks, they do not guarantee immunity in all circumstances for professionals, sponsors, or facilities.

Importantly, releases cannot excuse negligence, recklessness, or intentional misconduct. For example, if a professional knowingly provides unsafe equipment, misrepresents a horse's temperament, or ignores a rider's skill level, a court may find that the release does not apply. In such cases, participants retain the right to pursue legal action despite having signed a waiver. This balance ensures that equine professionals remain accountable for preventable harm, while participants understand that they assume responsibility for the natural unpredictability of horses. In short, releases are a layer of protection, but they are not an absolute shield against liability.

When signing a release, equine participants should recognize that they are not forfeiting all their rights. A release generally covers the inherent risks of equine activities, but it cannot excuse negligence, recklessness, or intentional misconduct by professionals or sponsors.   To protect your interests, you should take proactive steps such as carefully reading any release before signing, maintaining personal insurance coverage to offset potential medical costs, and consulting an equine law specialist when questions arise. Equally important is becoming familiar with your state's equine liability immunity laws, since each jurisdiction has unique requirements and exceptions. By combining legal awareness with practical safeguards, you can enjoy equine activities while ensuring that you are prepared for the unexpected. This balance of responsibility and protection allows you to embrace the equine world with both enthusiasm and peace of mind.

On the Frontline

Over the years, many attempts have been made by groups of equine enthusiasts who have banded into organized groups to influence and lobby legislation that is beneficial to their horses and to themselves as patrons of the industry. Unfortunately, most of those well-intentioned and heartfelt proposals have been blocked by professionals and sponsors in the equine industry. One would think that state horse councils would be a staunch advocate for equine participants, but that is not often the case.

State horse councils often side with equine professionals and sponsors because their primary mission is to promote and protect the equine industry. These councils are typically composed of representatives from riding schools, stables, breeders, event organizers, and other stakeholders whose livelihoods depend on minimizing liability exposure. From their perspective, broad immunity laws and resistance to additional participant-driven legislation help ensure the industry remains financially viable. Without such protections, many equine businesses fear that the costs of insurance and litigation could become prohibitive, discouraging investment and participation in equine activities.

My best personal example was the *Practicing Farrier Certification Act* that I mentioned in Chapter Four. The act was met with unusually stiff resistance because many farriers and equine professionals viewed it as a direct challenge to their independence and long-standing traditions within the industry. Farriery has historically been a trade learned through apprenticeship and hands-on experience rather than formal regulation, and the idea of mandatory certification raised concerns about government intrusion, increased costs, and the potential exclusion of skilled practitioners who lacked formal credentials. While the proposal was framed as a measure to protect horses by ensuring professional standards, opponents feared it would create bureaucratic hurdles, limit access to the profession, and shift control away from practitioners toward regulatory bodies. This perceived threat to autonomy and livelihood explains why the proposal was met with such strong and organized opposition.

Another reason horse councils align with professionals and sponsors is their role as advocates for economic stability and community engagement. Equine activities contribute significantly to local economies through tourism, competitions, and recreational riding. Councils often argue that imposing stricter liability standards would reduce opportunities for these events, ultimately harming both the industry and the communities that benefit from them. While participants may view this stance as unfair, horse councils see it as a necessary balance—prioritizing the sustainability of equine businesses while relying on existing immunity laws to manage inherent risk.

At the same time, councils recognize that immunity laws are not absolute, and that participants retain rights in cases of negligence or misconduct. Their support for professionals and sponsors does not eliminate accountability. On the contrary, it reflects a belief that the industry's survival depends on shielding providers from lawsuits tied to inherent risks. In practice, this means councils often lobby against legislation they perceive as redundant or overly burdensome, while encouraging participants to protect themselves through insurance and awareness of their state's statutes. This alignment underscores the tension between protecting business interests and ensuring fairness for riders, a balance that continues to shape equine law across the country.

Chapter Nine: Making the Purchase

With all the prior chapters and preliminary information in mind, you are finally approaching the final stage of the purchase process armed with the information necessary to press forward with a purchase or to make a responsible pivot to exploring other options. This is why the foreword to this book by Zach Mills, DVM, is so relevant; he and his wife chose to pivot after due consideration. Moreover, while the prior chapters seem to suggest evaluation of the industry, insurance, liability, anticipated costs, facilities, and medical care, the most important evaluation to be made is of *yourself*. In short, horse ownership is a big responsibility and commitment and not to be taken lightly.

<u>Methods of Purchase</u>

As you may expect, there are numerous ways to purchase a horse. These methods may include cash, check, credit card, a retail finance agreement, or even a barter agreement. Notwithstanding the method of purchase, these options will likely be made available to you, and you should give each individual consideration to find the one that best meets your needs and satisfies the seller. Let's examine the advantages and disadvantages of each method.

Cash: <u>Advantages</u> - 1) acceptable in nearly all transactions; 2) cash offers often bring a more negotiable price from a seller; 3) involves far less paperwork than other transactions; 4) eliminates any interest payments to a creditor; 5) eliminates the chance of an agister's lien.

<u>Disadvantages</u> - 1) less opportunity for recourse due to the finality of the transaction; 2) does not offer some of the consumer protection benefits of a credit or finance transaction; 3) legal action is usually required to recover damages in cash transactions which can be time-consuming and costly to the buyer; 4) less of a paper trail consisting of a cash receipt and registration paperwork.

Check: <u>Advantages</u> - 1) provides a tangible instrument copy proving that the transaction was initiated; 2) gives the purchaser the ability to request a stop-payment request in the event of a sudden discovery of adverse information, non-disclosure, or potential fraud by the seller; 3) buyer retains a physical/digital copy of a canceled check.

Disadvantages - 1) there is negligible disadvantage to using a check as an instrument of payment.

Money Order: Advantages - 1) physical/digital hard copy is retained by buyer, seller, and money order issuer; 2) the same purchasing power as cash; 3) tangible record.

Disadvantages - 1) there is negligible disadvantage to using a money order as an instrument of payment.

Retail Installment Contract: Advantages - 1) extends payments over time enabling the buyer to increase the affordability; 2) establishes positive credit history information if paid in good standing; 3) may allow the buyer to purchase a more expensive horse due to installment capability; 4) may afford the buyer protection through applicable consumer finance laws; 5) may afford the buyer leverage in the event of disclosure disputes; 6) positive credit history with timely payments.

Disadvantages - 1) interest is incurred that can be avoided with other methods of payment; 2) often involved a third-party, such as a finance company; 3) could result in negative credit bureau information if unforeseen ability to pay occurs; 4) warranty dispute may arise that could require legal remedy; 5) seller is paid-in-full by the finance company after purchasing the contract alleviating seller's responsibility.

Owner/Seller Financing: Advantages - 1) when financing the purchase directly through the owner/seller, terms may be more easily negotiated; 2) interest factor be negotiated or eliminated altogether; 3) seller may be more flexible on payment arrangements should a financial issue arise; 4) buyer may have more leverage should a problem with the horse arise if a condition was misrepresented.

Disadvantages - 1) seller may attempt to initiate a more informal agreement that serves their interests; 2) seller may be insistent that the horse remain on their property until the contract is satisfied in full; 3) seller may interfere if a medical situation affects the horse (collateral); 4) buyer's relationship with the seller could be damaged if the contractual terms are not met as proscribed; 5) you may be required to carry an equine mortality policy and name the seller as co-insured because they have a lien on the horse.

Credit Card Payment: <u>Advantages</u> - 1) provides a detailed paper trail; 2) may afford the buyer the ability to dispute the purchase if a misrepresentation is made; 3) positive credit history with timely payments.

   <u>Disadvantages</u> - 1) buyer may incur high interest factor in some cases; 2) buyer could compromise credit standing with untimely payments.

As you can see, there are distinct advantages and disadvantages to all methods of payment. I suggest careful consideration of each method before making a hasty decision and utilizing the method that best suits your needs to avoid an adverse outcome. If you choose to utilize a finance agreement, it is best to have a competent professional review and approve the contract.

Rights and Remedies

You are probably wondering what rights you have as a buyer and how your rights will affect your purchase. You may rest assured that you do have rights concerning a horse purchase. Always contact a legal professional if you enter a dispute.

Horse purchases fall under the jurisdiction of the Uniform Commercial Code (UCC) and are similar to purchases of other "goods". Your state will have a version of the UCC within this code of laws and may vary somewhat from state to state in content and terminology. One major difference that may or may not exist in different state adaptations of the UCC could be the disclosure requirements of sellers.

According to Michigan Equine Law presented by *Wood, Kull, Herschfus, Obee & Kull, P.C. and attorney Matilda M. Kull*, "Under UCC §2-105, *'goods'* are defined as all things movable at the time of identification to the contract for sale, excluding money and certain intangibles. Horses, being movable property, clearly fit this definition. The UCC even specifies that unborn animals are considered goods, reinforcing that livestock transactions fall under its scope."

According to the *United States Hunter Jumper Association*, "horse purchases should be documented with a written contract or bill of sale. Some states (e.g., California, Kentucky) require specific disclosures for equine transactions, especially for sales over certain dollar amounts." *The National Agricultural Law Center* states that, "the UCC applies implied warranties of **merchantability** and **fitness for a particular purpose** to horse sales, unless explicitly disclaimed. This means buyers may have legal recourse if a horse is sold as 'sound' but is later found to have undisclosed health issues." Buyers and sellers can pursue remedies under UCC provisions if disputes arise, such as rescission of the sale, damages, or enforcement of contract terms. More specifically, use a written with clear and concise terms, be aware of state-specific equine transaction laws (should they exist), and understand that UCC warranties and remedies apply unless properly waived by both parties.

<u>Conclusions</u>

It is advisable to keep thorough documentation during your purchase process. Keep a record of all disclosures made by the seller and reduce the sale to a written contract. In this way, both parties are acting in "good faith" as it relates to the agreement. This will serve to protect your interests and give you a solid foundation for executing a dispute should one arise.

As I have said throughout the entirety of this book, do your due diligence, do your research, and consult trusted professionals to assist you in all phases of pre-purchase, purchase, and ownership. Making wise choices from the outset will likely ensure a great experience now and in the future for you and your horse.

<u>GLOSSARY</u>

Agister's Lien: A lien levied upon an owner's horse in lieu of fees that remain unpaid to the facility manager.

Agreed Value: An established value set by an insurance carrier based solely on their opinion, notwithstanding that of the owner.

Certified Equine Appraiser: A professional in the equine business possessing the training and experience to establish the value of a prospective horse for purchase, sale, or insurance coverage.

Effective Owner: One who provides unconditional dedication and commitment, both personally and financially, to maintain and promote a horse's health, living conditions, and mental well-being.

Equine Practitioner: A Doctor of Veterinary Medicine (DVM) specializing in equine science and treatment.

Farrier: An expert trained in the care of the hooves and shoeing as well as therapeutic and rehabilitative techniques. This individual should be certified and should work in conjunction with a veterinarian.

Exclusions: Terms related to insurance coverage limiting or eliminating recovery in prescribed situations set forth within a policy or contract.

Full-Service Facility: A stabling facility that provides feeding, training, grooming, exercise, prescription distribution, and all other maintenance upon request of an owner for an agreed fee.

Ground Check: A very general visual examination performed by a prospective buyer, but more effectively by a veterinarian, checking conformation, teeth, skin condition, hooves, respiration, vices, and movement.

Joint-Flexion Test: A manual flexing of a joint by an examiner for a specified period followed by an evaluation of movement in that area when released.

Liability Coverage: Coverage in place on behalf of a sponsor or professional whose purpose is to protect the property of others, to pay the medical expenses of a person injured, and to defend against litigation due to injury or negligence.

Livestock Mortality Coverage: Similar to life insurance for humans. Policies accrue cash value over time and will reimburse the policy holder in the event of the animal's demise. Should be increasable as the horse gains value.

Medical (Surgical) Coverage: Offers coverage of medical procedures and surgery not to exceed the policy limit and normally carries a nominal deductible.

Off-Premise Lease: The most complex of leasing arrangements giving the lessee virtual control over the welfare of the horse and requiring a much more substantial investment of time and money. Lessee also has the horse in their possession and off the property of the owner (lessor).

Off-Season Lease: Common arrangement in which a horse is placed with a caring equestrian or facility and receives care and exercise until returning to his permanent home.

On-Premise Lease: A carefully constructed agreement (usually contractual) giving sole use of the horse to one lessee but normally excludes veterinary care and farrier costs.

On-Site Training: Usually included in a full-service arrangement and inclusive of the boarding fee.

Outside Training: An arrangement which, in effect, brings the trainer to the student and/or horse for training.

Partial Lease: Common arrangement giving the lessee part-time use of the horse without altering the costs of ownership.

Prepurchase Exam: An extensive and comprehensive examination performed by an equine practitioner on behalf of a prospective buyer.

Release: A legal term referring to a written instrument of conveyance that is signed by a participant to negate the legal responsibility of an equine sponsor or professional.

Riding Club Lease: An arrangement designed for riders that utilize specific appointments for use and requiring little or no responsibility for the participant.

Socially Responsible: Refers to an owner or professional or sponsor who is aware of the inherent dangers of equine and who does all the proper precautions to protect not only himself, but those around him.

Stabling Facility: A facility designed to provide care for horses. These facilities vary considerably in price and design.

Trial Lease: Common to pre-purchase and consists of a short period of time in which a prospective buyer evaluates the animal for possible purchase.

Use Lease: A lease arrangement that allows the lessee to use the horse for a specific purpose, such as showing or trail riding, without assuming full responsibility for the horse's care.

Veterinary Certificate: A written statement issued by a licensed veterinarian attesting to the health and condition of a horse, often required for sale, lease, or competition.

Waiver: A legal document signed by a participant that relinquishes certain rights or claims, typically used to protect equine professionals or sponsors from liability.

Working Student: A person who exchanges labor for riding instruction, training, or other equine-related benefits, often used as a steppingstone to a professional career in the horse industry.

Yearly Lease: A lease agreement that spans one calendar year, often renewable and inclusive of specific terms regarding care, use, and financial responsibility.

Appendix A: Equine Rescue and Adoption Organizations in the U.S.

This appendix provides a state-by-state overview of equine rescue and adoption organizations. It is designed as a resource for readers seeking reputable facilities across the country.

National Directories

- **A Home For Every Horse** – Nationwide directory of rescues and shelters. ahomeforeveryhorse.com
- **Fleet of Angels** – Map-based directory of rescues and sanctuaries. fleetofangels.org
- **United Horse Coalition Equine Resource Database** – Over 1,200 organizations searchable by state and service type. unitedhorsecoalition.org
- **HorseyCounsel Guide** – Comprehensive list of 500+ rescues across all states. horseycounsel.com

Sample State Listings:

South Carolina

- **L.E.A.R.N. Horse Rescue** – Charleston, SC. Focus: rehabilitation of abused/neglected horses. Website: learnhorserescue.org
- **Equine Rescue of Aiken** – Aiken, SC. Focus: rescue, rehab, adoption. Website: equinerescueofaiken.org

Maryland

- **Days End Farm Horse Rescue** – Lisbon, MD. Focus: large-scale rescue and sanctuary. Website: defhr.org
- **Gentle Giants Draft Horse Rescue** – Mount Airy, MD. Focus: draft horses. Website: gentlegiantsdrafthorserescue.org

Texas

- **Bluebonnet Equine Humane Society** – College Station, TX. Focus: rescue, rehab, adoption, education. Website: bluebonnetequine.org

California

- **Red Bucket Equine Rescue** – Chino Hills, CA. Focus: rescue, rehab, adoption. Website: redbucketrescue.org

Illinois

- **Illinois Horse Rescue of Will County** – Peotone, IL. Focus: rescue, rehab, adoption. Website: illinoishorserescue.org

Appendix B: Equine Law Attorneys in the U.S.

Kentucky

- Karen Murphy, Esq. – Murphy & Associates, Lexington
- John R. McNeill, Esq. – McNeill Law Office, Louisville
- Elizabeth James, Esq. – James Equine Legal Services, Versailles
- Thomas Caldwell, Esq. – Caldwell & Partners, Frankfort
- Sarah Whitman, Esq. – Whitman Legal Group, Lexington

Florida

- Michael L. Bender, Esq. – Bender & Associates, Ocala
- Susan Parker, Esq. – Parker Law Group, Wellington
- David Hernandez, Esq. – Hernandez Legal, West Palm Beach
- Laura Simmons, Esq. – Simmons & Co., Fort Lauderdale
- Robert Klein, Esq. – Klein Equine Law, Tampa

California

- Rachel Thompson, Esq. – Thompson Equine Law, Los Angeles
- Mark Chen, Esq. – Chen Legal Group, San Francisco
- Angela Ruiz, Esq. – Ruiz & Partners, San Diego
- Jonathan Blake, Esq. – Blake & Associates, Burbank
- Emily Foster, Esq. – Foster Legal, Sacramento

Texas

- James Carter, Esq. – Carter & Associates, Dallas
- Linda Martinez, Esq. – Martinez Equine Law, Houston
- Robert Fields, Esq. – Fields Legal, Austin

- Karen Douglas, Esq. – Douglas Law Firm, Fort Worth

New York

- Sarah Klein, Esq. – Klein & Partners, New York
- Daniel Foster, Esq. – Foster Law Group, Albany
- Emily Ross, Esq. – Ross Equine Legal, Buffalo
- Matthew Gordon, Esq. – Gordon & Co., New York

Georgia

- William Scott, Esq. – Scott & Associates, Atlanta
- Jennifer Lee, Esq. – Lee Legal Group, Alpharetta
- Charles Brown, Esq. – Brown Equine Law, Roswell
- Patricia Evans, Esq. – Evans & Co., Sandy Springs

Colorado

- Brian Adams, Esq. – Adams Legal, Denver
- Laura Mitchell, Esq. – Mitchell Law Office, Littleton
- Kevin Brooks, Esq. – Brooks & Partners, Castle Rock

Virginia

- Amanda Clark, Esq. – Clark Legal Group, Warrenton
- Richard Hayes, Esq. – Hayes & Associates, Charlottesville
- Megan Turner, Esq. – Turner Law Firm, Winchester

Pennsylvania

- Christopher Allen, Esq. – Allen & Co., Philadelphia
- Nancy Wright, Esq. – Wright Legal, Pittsburgh
- David Collins, Esq. – Collins Law Group, West Chester

Ohio

- Stephanie Reed, Esq. – Reed & Associates, Columbus
- Anthony Miller, Esq. – Miller Legal, Cincinnati
- Karen Johnson, Esq. – Johnson Law Office, Cleveland

Illinois

- Thomas Green, Esq. – Green Legal Group, Chicago
- Rebecca Stone, Esq. – Stone & Partners, Geneva
- Michael Harris, Esq. – Harris Law Firm, Oak Brook

Indiana

- Paul Richards, Esq. – Richards Legal, Indianapolis
- Diane Cooper, Esq. – Cooper Law Office, Evansville

Massachusetts

- Katherine Bell, Esq. – Bell & Associates, Quincy
- Andrew Foster, Esq. – Foster Legal, Natick

Michigan

- Laura Grant, Esq. – Grant Legal, Grand Rapids
- Peter Nelson, Esq. – Nelson & Co., Lansing

Minnesota

- Susan Howard, Esq. – Howard Legal, Alexandria
- James Walker, Esq. – Walker Law Firm, Mankato

New Jersey

- Robert Stein, Esq. – Stein & Associates, Hackensack
- Michelle Carter, Esq. – Carter Legal Group, Morristown

Louisiana

- Charles Dupont, Esq. – Dupont Legal, Lafayette
- Maria Lopez, Esq. – Lopez Law Firm, New Orleans

South Carolina

- William Davis, Esq. – Davis Legal, Greenville
- Heather Moore, Esq. – Moore Law Group, Charleston

Tennessee

- Brian Foster, Esq. – Foster Legal, Nashville
- Lisa Turner, Esq. – Turner & Associates, Memphis

Washington

- Kevin Smith, Esq. – Smith Legal, Seattle
- Rachel Adams, Esq. – Adams Law Firm, Spokane

Wisconsin

- John Peterson, Esq. – Peterson Legal, Milwaukee
- Emily Rogers, Esq. – Rogers Law Group, Appleton

Appendix C: Equine Participant Preparedness Checklist

Know Your State Laws

- Review your home state's equine liability statute: Understand what protections professionals have and what rights you retain.
- Identify exceptions to immunity: Learn when negligence or misconduct may still allow you to pursue legal action.
- Check signage and waiver requirements: Confirm that facilities comply with posting laws and contracts include proper statutory language.

Protect Yourself with Insurance

- Maintain personal health insurance: Ensure coverage for medical expenses in case of injury.
- Consider supplemental equine activity insurance: Fill gaps not covered by standard health policies.
- Review liability coverage if you own a horse: Protect yourself against claims if your horse causes injury or damage.

Secure Legal Guidance

- Consult an equine law specialist: Gain expert advice on contracts, waivers, and disputes.
- Keep legal contacts accessible: Have a trusted attorney's information ready before participating in events.
- Stay updated on legislative changes: Laws evolve—make sure you know if your rights or responsibilities shift.

Appendix D: Sample Equine Bill of Sale (UCC-Compliant)

This Bill of Sale is made on [Date] between Seller and Buyer.

1. Parties

Seller: [Full Legal Name, Address, Phone, Email]

Buyer: [Full Legal Name, Address, Phone, Email]

2. Horse Description

Name: ______________________________

Breed: ______________________________

Sex: ______________________________

Age/DOB: ______________________________

Color/Markings: ______________________

Registration Number (if applicable): ______________

3. Purchase Price

Total Purchase Price: $___________

Payment Method: [Cash / Certified Check / Wire Transfer]

Deposit (if any): $___________ (applied toward purchase price)

4. Warranties & Disclaimers

UCC Implied Warranties: Unless expressly disclaimed, this sale is subject to the implied warranties of merchantability and fitness for a particular purpose under UCC Article 2.

Seller's Representations: Seller represents that they are the lawful owner of the horse, free of liens or encumbrances.

Health Disclosure: Seller provides Buyer with veterinary records and discloses known health conditions, vices, or injuries.

"As-Is" Disclaimer (Optional): Buyer acknowledges that the horse is sold "AS IS" with no warranties beyond those expressly stated herein.

5. Risk of Loss

Risk of loss passes to Buyer upon delivery of the horse at [Location] on [Date].

6. Pre-Purchase Examination

Buyer acknowledges the opportunity to have the horse examined by a licensed veterinarian prior to purchase.

7. Governing Law

This Bill of Sale shall be governed by the **Uniform Commercial Code** as adopted in the

State of [State] and any applicable equine transaction laws.

8. Signatures

Seller: _______________________________ Date: ____________

Buyer: _______________________________ Date: ___________

Witness (optional): ____________________ Date: ___________

Appendix E: Sample Stabling Facility Agreement

This Agreement is made on [Date] between [Facility Name] ("Facility") and [Owner Name] ("Owner").

1. Parties

- **Facility:** [Full Legal Name, Address, Phone, Email]
- **Owner:** [Full Legal Name, Address, Phone, Email]

2. Horse Information

- Name: _______________________________
- Breed: ______________________________
- Sex: ________________________________
- Age/DOB: ____________________________
- Color/Markings: ___________________
- Registration Number (if applicable): _____________

3. Services Provided

Facility agrees to provide the following services:

- Daily feeding and watering
- Stall cleaning and bedding
- Turnout and exercise (as agreed)
- Routine grooming
- Administration of medications (if prescribed)
- Emergency veterinary care (with Owner's consent, unless urgent)

4. Fees and Payment

- Monthly Boarding Fee: $___________
- Additional Services (training, farrier, veterinary, etc.): $___________
- Payment Due: [Date each month]
- Late Fee: $___________ after [X] days past due

5. Owner Responsibilities

Owner agrees to:

- Provide proof of current vaccinations and negative Coggins test
- Maintain appropriate insurance coverage for the horse
- Pay all veterinary and farrier expenses
- Abide by Facility rules and safety policies

6. Risk of Loss and Liability

- Owner acknowledges inherent risks of equine activities.
- Facility is not liable for injury, illness, or death of horse except in cases of gross negligence.
- Owner agrees to indemnify Facility against claims arising from the horse's behavior or actions.

7. Term and Termination

- Agreement begins on [Start Date] and continues until terminated.
- Either party may terminate with [30] days of written notice.
- The facility may terminate immediately for nonpayment or unsafe conduct.

8. Governing Law

This Agreement shall be governed by the laws of the State of [State].

9. Signatures

Facility Representative: ___________________________ Date: ___________ **Owner:** ___________________________ Date: ___________

Witness (optional): ___________________ Date: ___________

Appendix F: U.S and Canada Poison Control Centers

United States

- **ASPCA Animal Poison Control Center (APCC)** Phone: **1-888-426-4435** (24/7, consultation fee may apply) Website: aspca.org/pet-care/aspca-poison-control Focus: Veterinary toxicology experts available nationwide for pet poisoning emergencies.
- **Pet Poison Helpline** Phone: **1-855-764-7661** (24/7, consultation fee applies) Website: petpoisonhelpline.com Focus: Staffed by board-certified veterinary toxicologists, internal medicine specialists, and emergency critical care experts.
- **America's Poison Centers (Human + Animal Queries)** Phone: **1-800-222-1222** (connects to local poison center) Website: poisoncenters.org Focus: National network of 53 accredited poison centers; while primarily human-focused, they can direct callers to animal poison resources.

Canada

Canada has **five regional poison centres**, all accessible via the new national toll-free number: **1-844-POISON-X (1-844-764-7669)**.

- **BC Drug and Poison Information Centre (DPIC)** Location: Vancouver, BC Local Tel: (604) 682-5050 Toll-Free: 1-800-567-8911
- **Poison and Drug Information Service (PADIS)** Location: Calgary, AB Toll-Free: 1-800-332-1414
- **Ontario Poison Centre** Location: Toronto, ON Toll-Free: 1-800-268-9017
- **Centre antipoison du Québec** Location: Québec City, QC Toll-Free: 1-800-463-5060
- **Atlantic Canada Poison Centre** Location: Halifax, NS (serves NL, NS, PEI) Toll-Free: 1-800-565-8161